The Destiny Formula

Find Your Purpose.
Overcome Your Fear of Failure.
Use Your Natural Talents and
Strengths to Build a Successful
Life.

Ayodeji Awosika

ISBN: 978-1522827-84-9

*This book is dedicated to Bobby Kalongo Jr.,
the person who is responsible for me
beginning my writing career.*

Contents

Introduction

We all have dreams and aspirations for our lives. Even if we are unaware of it, each of us has something that we are called to do. Each and every one of us is designed to walk our own distinct path and accomplish something that is unique to our personality.

We are very aware of this early on in our lives, but as time goes on, we may begin to lose sight of or completely forget our true calling. We're brought up to accept a certain set of rules and guidelines about how we are supposed to live. We slowly begin to believe that being different is somehow wrong and that we should follow the safe and secure path in order to have a good life.

We're given a narrative for the proper way to live life, and it goes something like this: "Go to school, get good grades, go to college, and find a safe and secure job afterwards." Many of us follow this prescribed plan, and it seems fine at first. We may find a job that provides a nice salary with benefits. We enjoy some of the luxuries that our job affords us, like having a nice home or driving a nice car. We seem happy and content, until one day, we're not.

After a while, we start to wonder if we've made the right choice. We might be working at a job that pays the bills but offers little to no meaning or engagement. We start to think about the dreams we used to have, and perhaps we even have regrets about not following them.

If this is you, then you've come to the right place. This book is for people who feel like there's more to life than the typical options laid out for them. This book is for people who want to truly live instead of merely exist.

The purpose of this book is to outline a strategy for figuring out what you really want to do with your life and giving you the right mindset to accomplish it.

This book is for people who have a dream they want to pursue but feel stuck and paralyzed. After reading this book, you'll be able to take the first step towards living the life of your dreams and create the momentum you need to finish what you've started.

I've spent hundreds of hours reading, learning, and implementing knowledge about what it takes to make your vision become a reality. Through this learning process, I've been able to glean insights from some of the most successful people in the world and compile that information to develop a strategy that will take you from a vague idea to concrete results.

People who have felt stuck and needed that extra push to finally pursue their dreams have used these strategies to become successful. Through these methods, they were able to discover their life's calling, create a plan, and turn their dreams into a reality.

I'll use myself as an example. My life was very different a year ago. I wasn't writing. I wasn't on the path to living a successful life. I wasn't doing much of anything really.

I started learning. I also sought a way to figure out exactly what I wanted to pursue. I decided that I wanted to be a writer and use words to help other people. It took me a little over a year, but using these strategies I'm about to share with you, I went from stuck in a dead end job to becoming a published author. If you follow these steps, you'll reach the goals you have too.

I'm not promising you that it will be easy, but what I am promising you is that if you listen to and implement what I'm about to share with you, you'll be well on your way to achieving anything that you want in life.

Don't be the type of person who ends up looking back at their life with regrets. Be the type of person that people admire because you've done what most people are unable to do: follow your dreams and do exactly what you set out to accomplish.

The techniques and strategies you're about to read have been proven to help people finally get over the hurdle and walk the path they were meant for.

Make the decision to create the circumstances you want for your life. Take the knowledge you gain from this book and implement it so that you're able to live your life exactly the way you want to.

To see more of my work visit: www.thedestinyformula.com

I also have some FREE bonus material for you to check out.

Visit www.thedestinyformula.com/bonus to get your free bonus content including ebooks, video series, and courses!

Chapter 1:
Finding Your Path

In this chapter, you're going to learn useful strategies to help you get a better idea of the path you're truly meant to follow. First, we'll go back to the beginning and discover what you were interested in as a child. Next, you'll learn how to listen to yourself and find the calling that lies deep within you. I'll show you how to discover your strengths and how to use your knowledge about yourself to sum up your path in just one sentence. At the end, you'll learn the approach you need to use going forward.

First Things First

The first step in your journey is to find the right path to follow. A great place to start is thinking about what you dreamed of being when you were a child. Children are open and expressive. They are more authentic and have a keener sense of their natural inclinations and preferences.

As we grow older, we start to receive input from outside sources that guide us into a certain path, which may or may not be true to who we really are. In order to rediscover the path you were meant to follow, you have to go back as far in your memory as possible to figure out where you should be headed going forward.

Think about what you were naturally drawn to as a child. Think of the things that really caught your interest. When I was a kid, I was drawn to books. I loved reading. Instead of my parents reading me bedtime stories, I would read stories to them. I've always had a natural curiosity for and interest in words. This is an example that you can use to start to get a better idea of what your interests were.

This may take a while. Your childhood memories may be vague, and it's possible that you have forgotten the subjects or ideas that you were drawn to as a child, but this is a step that you can't skip.

Take all of the time you need. Perhaps you need to sit in a silent room and really concentrate on your past. Even if it takes weeks or months, it's worth knowing.

The reason why you need to go back this far is because your childhood was a time when your thoughts were pure. You didn't have to worry about the pressures of society and the opinions of your peers. You could truly be yourself. Childhood is the time when you have the most creative energy.

Think about some of the things that children say. They're able to come up with these strange and unique notions about life because they aren't tethered to any kind of conventional wisdom. They see the world in a way that's not possible for adults. Going back to this source will not only help you find the right path to follow but also bring back the creative energy you need to pursue it.

If you can't think all the way back to your childhood, that's okay. You can use some of your early formative years as a guideline. Think back to your early teens. At that age, you were just beginning to learn more about available careers. You were still unencumbered and free to explore without pressure.

When I was in my early teens, I didn't necessarily think about being a writer, but I did think about working for myself and establishing my own company. I envisioned a life where I would be in charge. I had my mind set that I was going to do great things and that I wasn't going to be average.

Think back to your teenage years. What did you want to be? What did you think your life was going to look like in ten years? Does your reality now match what you thought back then? If not, the good news is that you still have the opportunity to change things and shape your life around your truest self.

When you grow older, you face more pressure to enter a career path for reasons that have little to do with our natural preferences. You may choose a type of career for the salary and prestige that it offers. You may have been influenced by the people around you to choose a certain career.

It might feel good for a while to have this type of job. If you're in a job that has a lucrative salary, you will enjoy some material benefits. If you're not careful, however, you may end up at a point in life where you feel stuck.

Life is okay, but it's not great. You have a decent job, but it's not very fulfilling. You'll start to wonder if you've made the right choice. You'll think about the dreams and aspirations you had when you were younger, and you'll regret not taking any chances.

What you do for a living is important. You will spend much of your life working. One of the keys to happiness is doing something for a living that you enjoy. Life is too short to be doing something you don't like just to pay the bills.

The good news is that it doesn't matter how long you've been traveling down a certain path. As long as you're alive, you have the opportunity to change directions. If you're just starting out in your career, you will have an easier transition. But even if you've been at it for a while, there's still time to pursue the path you were destined for.

No matter how far you've gone, the place to look for direction is at the beginning. Take some time to reflect on your earliest memories. Dive deep into your consciousness and rediscover the passion and interest you were born with.

Listen to Yourself

When it comes to discovering the path you were meant to follow, the decision rests with you and you alone. It's important not to let outside influences determine what you decide to do.

If I was to ask your childhood self what you wanted to be when you grew up, I doubt that you would say you wanted to be an accountant or a management consultant. We all have big dreams at the beginning of our lives, but as we grow older, limitations start embedding into our minds.

People you trust and look up to tell you that life has to be certain way. Oftentimes you're told what you can't do as opposed to what you can do.

Although they aren't trying to do harm, your parents can be one of the main sources of this limiting belief system being imposed on you. They care about you, love you, and want the best for you. But they aren't able to see life through your lens, and what they want for you may not be what you want for yourself.

They may suggest that you choose the same career that they have or one that seems safe and secure. They will most likely try to steer you away from anything deemed risky or unrealistic. This seemingly harmless advice can have a negative impact on your future.

If I could rewind my life and go back to the age of eighteen, I probably wouldn't have gone to college. At the time however, going to college wasn't one of several options, it was the only option.

My parents sent me to the best schools growing up. They wanted me to get good grades and get accepted to a prestigious university. The problem was that I never really enjoyed school. I was always an average student.

The way that school worked didn't make sense to me. Everyone was so worried about their grades but I always thought to myself, "this isn't going to matter much in the real world." I coasted along until it was time to apply for colleges.

They make you take standardized tests that colleges look at to find students that they want to recruit. I always did very well on those tests and as a result I had letters coming in from top universities around the country.

Harvard sent me a full application to fill out. I remember it being elaborate. My parents pestered me to fill it out, but I never did. My mother still brings up the Harvard application to this day.

I settled on a small school in Minnesota. It was the only one I applied to. I continued to be an average student. When I was done with my undergrad my parents suggested graduate school. I told them that I had no plans on furthering my formal education but it went in one ear an out of the other. Every time I talk to my dad on the phone he reminds me that I need to get my MBA.

If I had told them at eighteen that I wanted to skip going to college and start my writing career, they wouldn't have allowed it.

They mean well, but they just don't get it. That's okay. I've come to realize that when you are seeking to do something that's different, the people around you might not understand it.

You're the one who has to live your life. You're the one who has to decide what's right for you and go for it regardless of what the people around you think. It's up to you to have the courage to do something that most other people wouldn't.

Human beings by nature have the tendency to care about what other people think. This is due to the wiring of our brains. A long time ago in hunter-gatherer societies, social rejection meant alienation from the group, which ultimately meant death. Our brains haven't quite caught up to the conditions we live in now, so your brain actually believes that social rejection truly means danger.

Have you ever been embarrassed in front of a group of people? Your stomach probably tightened, you started breathing faster, and you may have begun to sweat. This social rejection caused your body to go into fight-or-flight response mode. The pain involved in being rejected in a social setting is far from trivial, but it's something you're going to have to overcome if you want to reach your destination.

If the path you've chosen deviates from the normal paths chosen by others, you have to be prepared for people trying to talk you out of it. They'll say things like "That's never going to work. Quit day dreaming." or "You have to be more realistic."

You have to understand that their opinions have everything to do with them and nothing to do you with you. When people tell you that what you're trying to achieve isn't possible, they're really just projecting their insecurity and limiting beliefs onto you. You can't allow that to stop you.

There's a lot of noise and distraction in the world. There will always be subtle influences trying to steer you off course. There are powers at work that are actively trying to keep you from pursuing your dreams.

If everybody decided to strike out on his or her own unique and individual path, then the structure of society would fall apart. Maintaining the status quo means making sure that people conform to the social norms of our society.

These influences have been acting against your true desires from the very beginning. Early on you learn that there are rules to be followed. You're taught to act a certain way. You're told to behave. You're put into neatly lined rows of desks where you're all taught exactly the same way regardless of the individual way you learn.

Your grand vision of the world can begin to narrow. When you were a child, you truly believed you could be an astronaut, a star athlete, or even president of the United States. But over time, you are left with only conventional options, and you are choosing from a prescribed list of careers.

Your parents, teachers, family, and friends will all try to convince you to do what they think is best, but deep down inside you may be feeling like there's something more to life than these cookie-cutter options. They know this deep down too, but it's difficult for most people to muster up the courage to admit it and do something about it. You have to be different.

You have the opportunity to strike out on your own path. You can make the decision to live the life you actually want to live. You can become a successful person that others look up to. You've been told all of your life that success is only reserved for a select few, but that's not true. Anybody can become successful.

We live in a society that treats highly successful people like they're anomalies. They'll attribute the good fortunes of these people to unnatural levels of talent or luck. What they'll never talk about is the fact that those people made a decision to be different, and they worked extremely hard to get there. Anyone who's accomplished something substantial has had to deal with people trying to steer them off course. It's all part of the game.

This is not to say that everyone is making poor choices when it comes to their careers. There are some people who are doing what they truly enjoy every day. But this is the exception, not the rule. For the most part, people have jobs they don't really like for no other reason than the belief they have to.

This way of thinking permeates our society, and it's affecting the people closest to you. Don't take it personally if they doubt you or talk negatively about what you hope to achieve. They can't help it. This way of thinking is lodged deep into their brains, and it's no small task to dislodge it.

But you're different. The fact that you are reading this book right now proves that you have a feeling that there's more to life than the options being laid out for you. I'll give you specific strategies to keep your mind focused on this journey, but the most important part is the beginning.

You have to accept the fact that most people just aren't going to get it. No one will be able to see your vision as clearly as you do. The path you've chosen can be a lonely one. People are going to try to convince you to quit. They may even laugh at you. You have to be tough, and you have to keep going no matter what they say. There's only one person who you should be listening to, and that's yourself.

Trust your gut. Believe in yourself. You're going to reach points in your journey where you'll feel like quitting, but you can't. Don't be the person who has to look back on their life with regrets, wondering what could have been.

Discovering Your Strengths

You've gone back to the beginning and took some time to reflect on your childhood interests and inclinations. You've decided to trust your gut and listen to yourself. Now it's time to refine your vision a little bit more.

One of the most important parts of formulating a clear vision for yourself is figuring out what you're good at.

People have the tendency to lean towards overconfidence in their abilities. If I asked you what you were good at, you'd probably have a number of responses for me. Most people think they're good at lots of things when in reality there are a few particular areas where they would be able to thrive. Your job is to find out what your natural talents are and develop a strategy to enhance them and turn them into strengths.

A great tool to help discover your strengths is the book *StrengthsFinder 2.0* that was created by the Gallup Research Company. This book comes with an access code to a questionnaire that will help you discover where your strengths lie. Through extensive research, they concluded that there are thirty-four distinct personality traits that people share.

The questionnaire takes about thirty to forty minutes, and afterwards you're able to read a report that outlines your highest-ranking personality traits. It gives you a detailed outline of each trait including a description of it, potential careers for people with the trait, and action items for you to use to improve on it and turn it into a true strength.

The Meyers-Briggs Type Indicator is another valuable tool to help you discover more about your personality. This questionnaire takes about ten minutes to complete. It breaks down your personality into four categories and paints an overall description. Many people swear by its relevancy, and from a personal standpoint, I think it's accurate.

There are several ways to help you figure out what talents you possess, and it's crucial that you figure out what they are. My advice to you is to focus solely on what you're good at and completely disregard the things you're bad at. There's no use spending any time trying to work on areas that you'll never be able to make significant improvements in.

This way of thinking is in exact opposition to the way that most people think about strengths and weaknesses. Think about what your parents would say to you about your grades every semester. You may have gotten high grades in several areas, but they'd likely focus on the few areas you did poorly in.

Why don't we help our young people focus on what they're good at so they can live fulfilling lives? There should be a lot more focus on aptitude in schools, but there isn't. You go to college and you have no idea what you're truly suited for so you decide on a path arbitrarily.

That's how you end up in a career you don't enjoy. That's how you end up unhappy and unfulfilled.

Your main goal should be to focus on your strengths and continue to cultivate them throughout your life.

You have to find an area where you think you can compete. You have to follow something I call the ninety percent strategy. The ninety percent strategy means that you should only pursue an area where you believe that you can eventually be in the top ten percent.

There are millions of basketball players in the world, but only about four hundred of them play in the NBA. There are tons of talented singers, actors, and entertainers, but very few of them ever see the limelight. In these arenas, being pretty good simply doesn't cut it.

What's an area you think you can compete in? Do you think that with diligence and effort you can one day be at the top of your field? If your answer is yes, then you're well on your way to starting the process, but if your answer is no, then you have to take some time to re-evaluate your choices and look at potential areas where you'll be able to thrive.

The key here is to be able to estimate your chances of being in the top ten percent *in the future*. You're not going to be able to reach the top overnight. It's going to take some effort on your part, but it is possible to consider whether you have a shot in the first place.

I'll use basketball again as an example. You may have a love for the game. You might even practice day and night. But if you're five foot two, your chances of making it to the NBA are slim to none. It's not likely that this is an area where you'll be able to compete.

We like to think that the world is full of options, but the truth is that it's better to be very good in one area than to be mediocre in several.

You probably think it's important to be well rounded. You're told that in order to find a good job, you must have a diverse résumé. It's great to gain experience and knowledge in multiple areas, don't get me wrong, but it's important to focus on an area that helps you highlight your strengths.

By now your vision of the path you're meant to follow should be a little less hazy than it was in the beginning. Next, we're going to do a practical exercise to really narrow things down some more.

Your One-Sentence Destiny

I want you to draw four circles that all overlap in the middle.

Each of these circles will represent a different category. Once you're finished, you'll see how they relate to one another, and it will help you get a clearer idea of what you should do.

In the first circle, I want you to write about your background and what your life was like growing up. I grew up middle class with two educated parents who were able to send me to private schools. Education is very important in my family.

Even if you didn't come from the best circumstances, you can still make good use of your past experiences.

Take Oprah for example. Oprah came from a dysfunctional home and suffered physical and mental abuse. On her show, she dealt with domestic issues and stories about people in disadvantaged situations. This is one of many examples of how your past (even a negative one) can be used as part of your destiny plan moving forward. What was your life like growing up? Write it down and be as specific as you can.

In the second circle, I want you to write about feedback from the people around you. You can use feedback from strangers as well as feedback from your friends.

Stranger feedback is what people compliment you on without you prompting them. Stranger feedback is useful because people who don't know you have no reason to lie to you, so the things that they compliment you on come from a genuine place.

I've always been told that I am articulate. I've been complimented on my ability to communicate. What do people say about you?

What are the things people consistently compliment you on?

You should also listen to feedback from your friends. What do your friends say you're good at? What are some things your friends find difficult to do that are easy for you?

You can go as far as to ask your friends what they think you're good at. Tell them that you're doing an exercise to help you get a better idea of what you're trying to pursue. Tell them to be serious. Ask them to name three to five things they think you truly have a talent for.

The people around you are leaving clues for you and you don't even know it. I like to talk a lot and share my opinions with other people. My friends come to me for advice and they trust me to give them guidance.

I've heard from the people around me multiple times that I should write a book, but I never gave it much thought until recently. Listen carefully to the compliments you receive. It's a great way to figure out what you should do going forward.

In the third circle, I want you to write about what you've been doing for a living for the past five years. Some of you might be wondering why this is important if you've been doing something that you don't like. Regardless of whether or not you liked what you've been doing for a living, you've most likely gained some skills along the way. My background is in marketing, sales, and customer service.

Even if you've been doing something like working at a fast food restaurant, you've still gained some skills from it. You need good communication skills to deal with different types of customers. You've probably mastered patience as a result of dealing with customers too. You also have to work with other people as a team in that type of job. No matter what the profession, there's always something of value to take away from it.

In the fourth and final circle, I want you to write down what you can talk about effortlessly. This section is for the things you'd talk to your friends about on a Saturday night with ease. I like to talk about ideas and creative ways of thinking and doing things. I talk with my friends about the future and the things we need to do to make it the best. I talk about ways that we can become better, learn more, and be more productive. What can you talk about effortlessly?

Take a look at your circles and how each of them overlaps in the center. Does it help you get a clearer picture of what you should be doing? We'll use mine as an example: I have an educated background. People tell me that I do a great job of communicating and writing. I have a background in marketing and sales, and I love to talk about ideas. I used the intersection of these to create my one-sentence destiny.

A one-sentence destiny is a way for you to sum up the path you're pursuing in one sentence. Summing up your goals this way gives you a clear sense of what you're after and makes it easy to communicate it with others. If you have a business and people ask you what the goal of your business is, it shouldn't sound overly complicated.

Let's say you're trying to pitch your new idea to an investor. These people hear dozens of pitches every day, so they're able to tell who knows what they're talking about pretty quickly. If you're not able to sum up your thoughts in a clear and concise way, they won't want to do business with you.

Forget about buzzwords and complicated terms. You need to be able to sum up your vision in a way that makes sense to everybody. Simple is the best way to go. If your sentence is over twelve words, then it's too long.

My one-sentence destiny is "Using words to liberate and enlighten others." It captures my goals and dreams in a way that's easy to understand. It also ties together what is represented in my circle graph.

I didn't just come up with that one sentence in five minutes. It started out as a paragraph, and I had to whittle away the unnecessary words until I was left with only what was needed. Take some time to create your one-sentence business destiny, and it will help you stay on track because you'll know exactly what you're after.

The Sculpture Approach

The final piece to your destiny puzzle is the approach that you should take going forward. Most people go about this by using the lottery approach to life. If you think and act with a lottery mentality, it's almost certain that you're not going to succeed.

The lottery approach is the idea that somehow, someway, things are just going to work out. You're relying on divine intervention to fix all of your problems instead of actually doing something about it.

This is a problem that a lot of people have. They're fixated on this imaginary situation where things fall into place with no effort. They look at people who are successful and figure they just got lucky or got their big break on accident.

This couldn't be further from the truth. Your chances of finding the good life this way are pretty much the same as winning the lottery. It's not going to happen. And besides, even if you did somehow get everything that you wanted with no effort, you wouldn't appreciate it.

Many lottery winners return back to their original level of happiness after a while. Some even lose all of their money and end up worse off than they were before. They've never had real money before, so they don't know how to handle it. If you earned millions of dollars through your own effort, you're less likely to spend all of it.

You should begin working towards your destination by using the sculpture approach. This is the way that successful people create the circumstances that they want.

Picture your dreams and aspirations as a large slab of stone. You have a general idea of what you want to do with your life from your one-sentence destiny. Your job now is to chip away at this stone until you have a beautiful sculpture.

You never change the rock itself, but you can try different ways to chip away at it. You can bounce around in different areas of your chosen industry as long as you stay in the general area. Try approaching it a certain way, and if it doesn't work well or doesn't suit you, try doing it a different way. You can attack a problem from lots of different angles.

Crafting a sculpture from a slab of stone takes time. It takes practice, effort, diligence, and skill. The sooner you realize that it's going to take you a while to get where you want to go, the better off you'll be.

We have a tendency to focus on the results and not on the process. You're ambitious. You want to reach your destination as soon as possible, but your lack of patience can end up being your worst enemy. The creative process can be a slow and tedious one. Settle in, get focused, and start chipping away.

The end of the road is the least important part of the journey. When you finally get what you want, the result itself won't be what makes you feel fulfilled. The memories of what you had to do to get there are what you're going to cherish.

"Go to bed a little wiser than you were when you woke up. Discharge your duties faithfully and well. Step-by-step you get ahead, but not necessarily in fast spurts. But you build discipline by preparing for fast spurts. Slug it out one inch at a time day-by-day. At the end of the day, if you live long enough, most people get what they deserve."—Charlie Munger

The number one reason you won't be successful is a lack of patience. Anything worth having takes time. What separates the mediocre from the great is the ability to stick with it. Think about it. Most of the people who've founded the world's most successful businesses started from scratch. They had to work tirelessly to get to where they are now. They slugged it out one inch at a time.

When a sculptor starts her work, it seems daunting, but slowly and surely the sculpture starts to form. The more invested she becomes in the work, the easier it becomes. She starts to see the different features developing, and with time, her methods become more refined.

In the end, she's left with a marvelous sculpture that will be a display of her efforts for everyone to see. She doesn't simply marvel at her creation. She remembers all of the work that it took to create it.

You have to treat your life this way. Treat each day like the sculptor treats her rock. You're not trying to do it all at once. You're just chipping away, and you keep chipping away until all that's left is a masterpiece.

You've learned how to find the right path by going back to your childhood and listening to yourself. You've also learned how to discover your strengths and be able to sum up your business destiny plan in one sentence. You've also learned how to use the sculpture approach to refine your vision until it's crystal clear. In the next chapter, you will learn how to develop the right mindset to have when you embark on the journey to fulfill your life's purpose.

For free bonus material visit:
www.thedestinyformula.com/bonus

Chapter 2:
Developing the Right Mindset

In this chapter, you will learn about the most important factor of success. You will learn to harness the power of thinking big. You will learn how to use contrast to make your goals seem more achievable. You will learn to develop a stoic attitude and delay your gratification. You will also learn how to make the right choices and be the best in everything that you do.

Do You Deserve It?

"To get what you want, you have to deserve what you want. The world is not yet a crazy enough place to reward a bunch of undeserving people."—Charlie Munger

We're going to go over several different mindsets and strategies to help you get where you want to go, but if you don't get this part right, there's no use in continuing. This is the foundation of success. It's the motto that all high level achievers live by. To get what you want, you have to deserve what you want.

Many people are dissatisfied with their lives. Things just don't seem to be going their way. They may attribute it to bad luck, the economy, their employers, or whoever they can to ignore the reality of the situation. People who think this way are not following the rules of success. They don't realize that they have to deserve it.

Let's use Bill Gates for example. Now you may not agree that he deserves quite as much as he makes, but you have to admit that he has earned his position. With extremely hard work and dedication, he created something that changed the way we live our lives. He was rewarded for his effort with billions of dollars.

If you haven't made the sacrifices necessary to reach the level of success you're trying to achieve, you have no one to blame but yourself. The only way to get what you want is to be worthy of having it.

Maybe you want to be wealthy. For many people, making a million dollars is a benchmark for wealth and status. Let's break things down a little bit to see how much value you have to provide to make a million dollars. Assuming you worked fifty hours per week, you would have to make about $385 per hour in order to make a million dollars in a year. Is an hour of your time worth $385 to anyone? If the answer is no, then there's no reason for you to be upset that you're not making a million dollars.

Deserving what you want means being able to provide something that's valuable and in demand. Being able to provide something valuable is a result of the skills you develop and creating a strategy to deliver that value.

We're all talented in one way or another. You've already taken the time to create a vision for your life and for your future. Now it's time to start working on making it a reality. It's not enough to be talented. There are millions of talented yet unsuccessful people. The reason they're unsuccessful has little to do with circumstances and everything to do with ignoring this cardinal rule. They don't think that they have to deserve it.

It doesn't matter how nice or well intentioned you are. Everybody has a story for why they're not where they want to be, and they don't want to hear yours. At the end of the day, the only person who is responsible for your well-being is you.

Ignore this advice and you'll continue to live how you've always lived, and things will never change. It's uncomfortable to acknowledge the fact that you're the reason why things aren't going well. It's hard to admit that you have no one else to blame. But it's the only way to free yourself and have a chance to make an impact.

So, how do you deserve it?

You deserve it by building knowledge and increasing your skill set. People who run successful companies have knowledge. It didn't happen by accident either. They made a decision to learn what they needed to learn to be successful in their industry. Even people who are naturally gifted have to work hard to deserve it.

I'll use one of the most well known athletes of all time as an example: Michael Jordan. When people think of Michael Jordan, they attribute his success on the basketball court to genetics. They say he can't be a human being with his skills. While he's obviously gifted, the reason why he became the greatest basketball player ever had much more to do with his work ethic.

I read his biography, and the one thing nearly everyone had to say about him was that he worked harder than anyone else. He was the first one to show up to practice and the last one to leave. He pushed his teammates to the limit and gave them no choice but to give a maximum effort. You didn't play on a team with Michael Jordan and slack off.

He wasn't always the Jordan we remember though. He was cut from his high school basketball team, and he wasn't even highly recruited once he graduated. During college, people saw that he was talented, but no one imagined that he would become the greatest basketball player of all time. He was picked third in the NBA draft. He exploded onto the scene and captivated audiences across the nation, but that was after he'd been consistently practicing for a decade. And by consistent, I mean *every single day of his life.*

Keeping with basketball, I'll give you an example of someone who was naturally talented but ended up going nowhere.

I watched a documentary about a basketball player named Lenny Cooke. He was the number one ranked high school basketball player at the time, even above LeBron James. If you're not too familiar with basketball, LeBron James is one of the top players in the NBA today.

Lenny had the potential to become great. Scouts and recruiters marveled at his natural athletic ability and feel for the game. But Lenny had one problem—he wasn't disciplined.

He assumed that because he was gifted he didn't have to work hard. He figured that he was guaranteed to be a top draft pick.

Due to him turning nineteen his senior year, he wasn't allowed to play high school basketball anymore. People suggested that he use that year off to attend a prep school to play basketball or to keep up with his workouts so that he would be in top shape come draft time. He did neither. When draft time came around, his name wasn't called.

He ended up playing overseas for a while, but ultimately, his basketball career fizzled out. The end of the documentary shows him sitting on the couch watching an NBA game. He's overweight and unemployed. He remarks that his son's favorite basketball player is LeBron James.

These examples illustrate the powerful effect of deserving what you want. You're not guaranteed anything in life. You can have all the talent in the world, and it will go to waste if you don't make an effort to build on it.

You deserve it by being able to stick with things and never giving up. Colonel Sanders, famously known for being the founder of KFC, didn't achieve business success until his 60s. He had attempted dozens of businesses and failed.

He could have decided that he wasn't cut out for business after all of those failed attempts, but he didn't. Even when he came up with the idea for KFC, he was turned down by hundreds of investors before finally finding someone to back him. That's deserving what you want.

You deserve it by being tough and not complaining. Many people complain about what they don't have, but they don't do anything about it. Let's say you're broke, and you want more money.

Have you taken the time to learn how to make money? You can't have what you don't know. You can go to the library right now and go to the finance section and pour through the material over and over again until you have it down. But that's just too much work, right? Enjoy staying broke.

Let's say you want to get in better shape. It's not a mystery. You know what you need to do. You have to eat right, and you have to exercise. It's simple. If your metabolism is slower than others, you're going to have to work harder. There's nothing you can do about it except work. But that's just too difficult, right? Enjoy being unhealthy.

This is the law you have to live by. Any time you're feeling discouraged or you feel like complaining, you have to remember this foundational rule: To get what you want, you have to deserve what you want.

The Magic of Thinking Big

There is magic in thinking big. The size of your dreams is what ultimately decides your future. The more you're able to stretch the size of your thinking, the more you'll be able to accomplish. One of the main reasons why people don't succeed is because they set limitations on what's possible.

They say things like "You have to be realistic." or "It's just not in the cards for me." They've set a ceiling for their accomplishments, and they'll never be able to achieve more than what their limiting beliefs allow them to.

I read about an interesting experiment that was done with fleas. If you didn't know, fleas are quite the athletes. They are microscopic in size, but they're able to jump multiple feet in the air. In the experiment, they took a group of fleas and put them in a jar. They quickly jumped out of the jar.

The experimenter then put a lid on the jar. The fleas jumped and jumped, hitting the lid several times. After a while, however, the fleas were conditioned to jump only as high as the lid would allow them to. The experimenter took the lid off, and the fleas continued to jump only to the height of the lid, even though it was removed. This is what people do in real life.

The influences around you have been trying to condition you to jump only as high as the lid allows. You're told to find a safe and secure job (lid). You're told to be realistic (lid). You're told that only the extremely intelligent and talented are able to succeed (lid).

The good news is that the lid isn't real. It's imaginary. The limits you put on yourself have nothing to do with reality. It's all in your head. You have a choice. You have the power to decide that you want to live a life with no limits. You can jump as high as you want to.

What do you think your ceiling is? If you had to guess how much potential you actually have, would you be able to come up with a concrete answer? I doubt it. The reality is that nobody knows what their ceiling is. What ever you think you're capable of, you're probably underestimating it. Your dreams probably need to be ten times the size of what they are right now.

The people you look up to—company founders, entertainers, and influencers—are just people. There's only one area of their body that works differently than yours-their brain.

It's easy to look at the founders companies like Google, Apple, Facebook, or YouTube and say, "those guys are geniuses. I could never do anything like that." What you forget is that at one point these mammoth companies were just ideas.

You can't compare yourself to people who have already reached the Promised Land. You have to remember that at one point they were just starting out, and nobody knew who they were. They had to think big to get where they are now.

Living big is the only way to reach your true work potential and experience the life you were meant for. Small thinking leads to small results. Placing limits in your mind creates limits in your life.

The things you think become a self-fulfilling prophecy.

I've noticed a theme in our society that trying to do something great is somehow selfish. Wealthy and successful people are scoffed at and called greedy.

Many people take pride in being average, and they'll say things like "Money doesn't matter." or "I have a family to take care of, and I can't afford to do anything risky." This is a cop out. It's a defense mechanism that people use so that they don't have to admit the truth. The truth is that they just don't have the guts to do it. They're scared and paralyzed by fear.

They fear their own power. They fear their potential.

In this beautiful poem, Marianne Williamson describes this fear that many of us share:

Our greatest fear is not that we are inadequate,
but that we are powerful beyond measure.

It is our light, not our darkness that frightens us.
We ask ourselves, who am I to be brilliant,

gorgeous, handsome, talented and fabulous?

Actually, who are you not to be?
You are a child of God.

Your playing small does not serve the world.
There is nothing enlightened about shrinking
so that other people won't feel insecure around
you.

We were born to make manifest the glory of
God within us.
It is not just in some; it is in everyone.

And, as we let our own light shine, we
consciously give
other people permission to do the same.
As we are liberated from our fear,
our presence automatically liberates others.

You're not doing anyone any favors by thinking small. You were put on this earth to do amazing things. You have a purpose. You're destined to be great. You just have to believe it.

If your dreams don't scare you a little bit, they're not big enough. What's the point in creating an imaginary limit for yourself? It won't make you feel better, and it won't keep that nagging feeling of regret from eating away at your soul. Mark my words—if you don't aim high and accomplish the goals and dreams you have, you're going to regret it.

I'm not saying that achievement is the only important part of your life. Your relationships with other people are more important than money or success. Life is filled with many precious little moments. But we are wired to achieve and seek significance. It's in our DNA.

If you set the right time frame, anything is realistic. You can set your sights high in the long term, but you do have to be realistic about what goes on in the short term. Becoming an overnight success is rare.

You have to constantly remind yourself that you're better than you think you are. You have to allow big thinking to dominate your thoughts. When opportunity arises, you have to think "I can" and not "I can't." You have to set extremely high goals for yourself if you want maximum results.

You have to believe in yourself, and you can't allow the limiting opinions of others hold you back.

"People who tell you it cannot be done almost always are unsuccessful people, strictly average, or mediocre at best in terms of accomplishment."—David J. Schwartz.

Ignore the crowd and decide that you're going to live life on a larger scale. Use your imagination to create the future you've always dreamed of. You have to visualize your success everyday and always be pushing towards the future.

You have to think big.

The Contrast Strategy

If you still need some more insight to help you think on a larger scale, I have a strategy that will help you put your goals into the right perspective. It's called the contrast strategy. The contrast strategy involves taking something incredibly difficult and comparing it to what you're trying to accomplish.

One example can use for contrast is man landing on the moon.

It took billions of dollars and the concentrated effort of a large group of scientists, but we figured out how to put man on the moon. Compared to this achievement, how difficult is the goal you're trying to accomplish?

If they put man on the moon, can you

- make a million dollars;

- write a book;

- start your own business;

- invent a new product; or

- (Insert your goal here)?

The answer is yes. Any time you're struggling with a task that seems daunting or a goal that seems unreachable, use the contrast strategy to help you realize that it can be done.

If the man on the moon example isn't enough for you, here are a few more achievements in human history that will make your goal seem more reachable:

1. Learning how to fly—Man dreamed of a flying machine for hundreds, if not thousands, of years. The Wright brothers developed their mechanical knowledge for more than a decade, and their creativity and ingenuity led to an event that would change the world. On December 17, 1903, they sustained the first heavier-than-air human flight.

2. Helen Keller's life—Helen Keller lived the majority of her life without the ability to see or hear, and she authored several books. These weren't just mediocre books either. She authored masterful pieces of literature without the sensory capabilities of most people.

3. Stephen Hawking studying the universe from his wheelchair—In his early twenties, Hawking was diagnosed with ALS. Instead of letting this debilitating disease limit his achievements, he went on to make groundbreaking discoveries in science. With most of his motor capabilities deteriorated or absent due to his disease, he wrote books by moving the muscles in his cheek. He wrote a book detailing a theory to describe the entire universe *with his cheek*.

4. Bill Gates and the ten dark years—Many of us see the finished product that is Bill Gates, but the billionaire computer aficionado wasn't always at the top of the Forbes list. He was quoted as saying, "During my twenties, I never took a day off." That's 3,650 days of excruciating mental work in a row. How many days

in a row have you worked towards reaching your goal?

5. Elon Musk betting it all—Elon Musk is the only person in the world who owns three separate billion-dollar companies. He netted more than one hundred million dollars from the sale of PayPal and subsequently reinvested nearly *all of his money* to create SpaceX, Solar City, and Tesla Motors. Talk about having faith in your dreams. Think about this when you are worried about potentially losing money you invest into a business endeavor.

6. Thomas Edison creating the light bulb—The estimates on how many failed attempts Edison made to create the light bulb ranges from one thousand to ten thousand, depending on whom you ask. That's a ridiculous amount of perseverance. How many of us would have given up after the tenth try? How about the hundredth try? Keep working until you get what you desire.

7. Nelson Mandela liberating South Africa—Nelson Mandela was a political activist who fought to abolish apartheid

in South Africa. He was arrested for conspiracy to overthrow the South African government. He then spent twenty-seven years in prison. He was released from prison, went on to become the president of South Africa, and won the Nobel Peace Prize. Many of us will give up on our dreams after a couple of years. Mandela maintained faith in his mission for nearly three decades. That's persistence.

These are just a few of many examples of people who combined big thinking, creativity, persistence, and patience to accomplish amazing things. Anything you're trying to attempt is possible. The word *impossible* shouldn't be in your vocabulary.

If they put man on the moon, what are you capable of?

The Stoic Attitude

The next piece of the puzzle you're going to learn is an important one. It's the one that trips people up the most.

You have to develop a stoic attitude. Nearly everyone who becomes successful in any area follows this strategy for success.

I'm not going to dive deeply into the details of stoic philosophy because that would entail writing an entirely separate book. In essence, being stoic means being able to forgo present pleasure to receive a benefit in the future. It's the ability to delay your gratification.

When you attempt to accomplish something you've never done before, you're going to run into moments where you wish things were developing more quickly. You want to make a name for yourself as soon as possible, and you can become impatient if you don't get results right away. If you don't learn how to delay your gratification, you'll eventually grow tired of the work and give up.

The problem of wanting instant gratification can be seen in many different areas. You live in a society that promotes pleasure seeking and instant results. Following this way of thinking and living is a surefire way to keep you from achieving anything substantial.

One example of how instant gratification causes harm is with our bodies. Many Americans are overweight and obese. The average American may eat at fast food restaurants multiple times in a week. It's pleasurable to eat unhealthy foods. The neurons in the pleasure centers of your brain are firing when you eat that delicious cheeseburger, and you feel happy. One cheeseburger isn't going to kill you, but too many of them over a lifetime might.

Another area where this comes into play is your personal finance. Most of us will make well over a million dollars in our lifetime, but few of us will become millionaires. The problem has more to do with what you keep than what you make.

If you were committed and consistent, becoming wealthy would be inevitable. Given enough time to use compound interest to make your money grow, you would eventually become rich using a passive investing strategy, but that's not what most people do.

We live for today, and we buy things we don't need to impress people that we don't even like. You make a choice daily with your spending habits. If you chose to delay your gratification, you'd be able to become financially independent.

It might be hard for you to look at the bigger picture, but you have to play the long game when it comes to being successful. You have to keep your vision in mind and continue to push forward until you get where you need to be. Be quick but not in a hurry.

There are two different ways to look at life. There's the stoic attitude and the epicurean attitude. The basic motto of the epicurean attitude is "Eat, drink, and be merry." This attitude says that you should pay no attention to the future and just live for the present moment. Most people have this attitude. It's the reason why most people aren't living the lives they truly want to live.

When you live for the present only, you're never able to build a solid foundation for the future. You always have to do more to be able to fulfill your desires. This is how people get stuck in the rat race.

The rat race is the process of continuously having to work to pay your bills. People don't live within their means, so they continue to have to earn more to feed their consumption needs. When you're in the rat race, you're like a hamster on a wheel that's constantly running but going nowhere. That isn't a life you want to live.

When you have a stoic attitude, you're able to put in the necessary effort without receiving any immediate pleasure, and your reward in the future is going to be ten fold. You're going to have to make sacrifices, but it's going to be well worth it.

Success isn't linear. It's not a simple process of climbing a ladder one rung after another. Success is exponential. Each time you put in effort, it builds exponentially, until one day it explodes. Remember the quote from Charlie Munger earlier in the book: "Step-by-step you get ahead, but not necessarily in fast spurts. But you build discipline by preparing for fast spurts." Persistence separates the average from the great. Your fast spurt will come, and since you've been preparing for it, you'll have the skills you need to take your life to the next level.

It's not about brains or talent; it's about commitment. There are going to be days when you feel like giving up, but you can't. There will be times when it seems like your efforts are in vain and you're getting no results, but that's not true. Every day that you spend working diligently brings you closer to your destination. Even if you make mistakes along the way, you're able to learn from them.

You have a decision to make. You can live for the present and waste a bit more of yourself each day until you wind up regretting your life, or you can decide that you're going to do what it takes now to reap massive rewards in the future.

The choice is yours.

It's All About Choices

Every moment of your life involves a choice. You make millions of decisions in your lifetime, and those decisions are what lead to the type of life you have. To be successful, you need the ability to make the right decisions.

Life isn't stagnant. You're always moving in a certain direction based on the choices you make. You're either moving closer to your dreams or further away from them. You need to become more aware of the choices you make every moment, and you have to understand the impact they're having on your life.

"What you build today will either empower you or restrict you tomorrow."—Gary Keller.

What are you building today? Is it empowering you or restricting you? Are you making the right choices? What type of habits are you forming?

Let's say you want to get in better shape. You have to make choices everyday that are going to take you closer to being healthy or push you further away from it. You have to make decisions about what you put into your body. Each time you eat something nutritious, that's a point in the win column. You arguably lose multiple points each time you eat something that's unhealthy.

You have a day planned where you're supposed to hit the gym. Do you go, or do you blow it off? You have a choice.

Underachievers' favorite words are "next time," "tomorrow," and "eventually." You can keep pushing things off, but one day, it's going to be too late. What you don't realize is that the further away you get from your goals, the harder it becomes to take action.

The more out of shape you get, the harder it is to get back in shape. Bad habits are extremely difficult to shake. Your choices can be steps towards the top or nails in your coffin. If you make enough bad choices, you'll end up leading a life of resignation.

Resignation works like this. You start with a positive outlook for your life. You make a couple of bad choices, so it makes things harder to achieve. You make more bad choices because you've developed bad habits.

These bad habits hard wire themselves into your brain until one day it becomes nearly improbable to make a significant change in your life. You simply say to yourself, "Forget it. This is the way my life is going to be, and there's nothing I can do about it." That's resignation.

I see people who appear resigned all of the time. The best place to find them is on the freeway every Monday morning. Do you ever notice that most of the people driving to work look miserable? You can see the slight twinge of desperation and the agony in their faces. They've made up their minds that there's nothing they can do to change their circumstances. Monday is going to be the worst day of the week for the rest of their lives.

You can't let this happen to you. It's still possible to make a change at any point in your life, but some situations are harder to get out of than others. Since you're reading this book, I'm assuming that you're someone who wants more out of life and hasn't given up completely, but even if you're close to resignation, there's still a way out.

You can make a decision now. The Latin root *cis* in *decision* means, "to cut off." When you make a decision to do one thing, you're cutting off your other options. So, decide right now that you're going to give a damn about your life. Decide that you're going to do what ever it takes to turn your dreams into reality. Decide that you're sick and tired of living a life that's going nowhere.

You have a choice between building someone else's dream for them and building your own. Choose yourself.

Purpose and Priority

A life without purpose is powerless. If you don't have a greater purpose to what you're doing day in and day out, you won't be motivated enough to follow through. Your purpose is the reason you do what you do every day.

A great way to figure out your purpose is to start with why. Simon Sinek wrote an amazing book called *Start With Why* that talks about how successful people and organizations use the word *why* to get results.

I'm paraphrasing Sinek's sentiments here, but the reason why many people feel lost is because they have no purpose for their lives. They have no *why* behind what they do every day. They're just going through the motions.

Until you have a solid *why* behind what you do, you'll always fall short of your goals. Your *why* is what you go back to when you're feeling discouraged. It's what you go back to when you start to lose perspective. It's the source of all of your energy and power.

Earlier in the book, we used a couple of different strategies to help you choose your "rock," or area of interest that you're going to pursue to reach your destiny. Why did you pick that subject? What greater purpose is it going to serve? Dive deeply into your *why*. The clearer your vision, the easier it will be to push forward.

The reason why I chose to follow the path that I'm on now is because I want to help other people see that there's more to life than being ordinary. I've always felt like there was something wrong with the normal way of doing things. Now it's my mission to help as many people as I can find their purpose in life.

When you have a purpose for your life, you have to prioritize certain things over others. When you act out of priority, your life is going to become unbalanced. It seems counter intuitive, but having an unbalanced life is a *good thing*.

There are tons of books and articles that promote a balanced life. They talk about finding the proper work/life balance and how to juggle all of the other obligations you have. But trying to lead a balanced life is the wrong approach to take.

You have to make time for your family and close friends of course, but aside from that, all of your energy needs to be poured into your purpose, ignoring everything else. You have to learn how to focus on what you need to accomplish and say no to anything that isn't important.

You have to be frugal with your time. Time is the most important resource in your life. It's ten times more valuable than money. You have to be conservative with your energy as well. You only get so much of it.

We are much too generous with our time. We feel obligated to say yes to every invitation and lend a hand to anyone who's in need.

You do this because you're a nice person. You do this because you don't want to upset anyone. But when you try to please everybody, you'll end up miserable.

There are a lot of different influences that are trying to pull you away from your purpose. It's easy to get distracted. When you act out of priority, you block out the noise of the world and focus on what needs to be done. You're not going to get very far without focus.

You can either be great in one area or mediocre in many. You've chosen your destination, and now you have to stick to it. It's okay to play around with different strategies and experiment with different ways to get there, but you have to keep your aim in the same area.

People without priorities are busy, which is just another word for inefficient. When someone says they're busy, they mean that they're busy doing a lot of unimportant things. People who are obstinate about their destination aren't busy; they're purposeful.

Stop being busy. Start acting out of priority.

Do What You Do and Do It Well

The final part of having the right mindset is to always be the best at what you do. You owe it to yourself and to the people you work with to give a maximum effort all of the time.

Even if you're not quite where you'd like to be, it's not an excuse for you to slack off. You can't have a sense of entitlement if you want to be successful.

Let's say you are underemployed, meaning that you aren't making the kind of money that you feel you deserve. You can blame the economy, your employer, or whomever else you can for your position in life. As a product of those negative thoughts, you exhibit habits and behaviors that cause you to slack off while you are at work. After all, this job is beneath you, so why would you try hard? These behaviors prevent you from advancing.

You can be in a similar situation but have a completely different attitude. You're underemployed, but you have a positive attitude. You give it your absolute best every time you're there. Your supervisor notices your hard work, and you get promoted.

See where I'm going with this? In order to change anything that's on the outside, you have to start by making changes on the inside. Some people will wish for a better life, but they never strive to make themselves better and then wonder why their life isn't going anywhere.

When you do everything that you do well, you attract positive outcomes. You get what you give in life. The universe will respond to you in a positive way if you're always giving it your best. When you pride yourself on your performance in everything that you do, it's noticeable. You'll have a completely different presence and people will feel it when they're around you.

"Practice doesn't make perfect. Only perfect practice makes perfect."—Vince Lombardi

When it comes to doing what you do well, everything is important. You might have a sound strategy, but is the way you're implementing it refined enough? Nothing is insignificant. Treat each moment of your life like practice and make sure that you're practice is as close to perfect as you can make it.

You've learned that in order to get what you want you have to deserve that you want. You've also learned the importance of thinking as big as you possibly can. You have learned how to develop the stoic attitude of delaying your gratification. You've learned that if they can put man on the moon, then you can do practically anything. You've also learned the power of decision making and doing the best work you can no matter what your job is. In the next chapter, we are going to talk about building knowledge and developing skills that are going to be critical to your success going forward.

For free bonus material visit:
www.thedestinyformula.com/bonus

Chapter 3:
The Importance of Building Knowledge

In this chapter, you're going to learn the necessity of committing to a life of continuous learning and development. You're going to learn about the power of curiosity as well as how to think more fluidly. You're going to learn how to become more observant and use your observations to go into a state of deep thinking about your life. You will also learn how to remove ignorant beliefs and mindsets that will keep you from reaching your goals.

Lifelong Learning

You should be starting to feel more confident and have a clearer vision for the path you want to follow. The next step is developing the necessary knowledge that will help you get ahead.

The first step in building knowledge is to make a commitment to a continual learning process for rest of your life. A common trait among highly successful people is an insatiable appetite for learning. They realize that the more they learn, the less they really know, and that's because there's a whole lot to know.

The more you learn, the more you'll potentially earn. One of the main things that separate the top one percent from the rest of the crowd is expert level knowledge.

I'll use billionaire investor Warren Buffet as an example. From a very early age, Warren knew that he wanted to be an investor. When he was a child, he went to the public library in his hometown and started reading books about investing and finance. *He read every finance book they had in the library more than once.*

He continued to read and learn for the rest of this life, and he still learns at the same pace to this day. He is said to read up to eight hours per day, every single day. His business partner, who also happens to be a billionaire, has this advice about learning:

"Without lifetime learning, you are not going to do very well. You are not going to get very far in life based on what you already know. I constantly see people rise in life that are not

the smartest, sometimes not even the most diligent, but they are learning machines. They go to bed every night a little wiser than they were when they got up, and boy does that help, particularly when you have a long run ahead of you."—Charlie Munger.

Oftentimes people attribute genetics and talent to success, but the reality is that with a dedication to learning and skill development, you can be just as successful as somebody more talented than you, if not more.

There are tools and resources that are readily available to all of us that can be used to build a solid knowledge base. My favorite resource is reading books. Books are dollar for dollar the best investment you can make in your own education.

The great thing about a book is that all of the research is done for you. The author may have spent years or even decades compiling useful information, and then he or she puts it into a book that you can read in a couple of hours. The power of reading allows you to implement the knowledge of some of the smartest people who have lived.

There are a couple of different types of books that will help you on your journey of lifelong education.

- The classics—These are books that have stood the test of time. As a rule of thumb, this type of book should be at least fifty years old, preferably one hundred years or more. These books are great resources because they've continued to stay relevant over a long period of time. You need to know the classics to have a solid foundation to build from.

- How-to books—These are books that usually focus on self-development and tend to be more business related. You can look for these types of books by top professionals in the industry you're trying to learn more about. These are important because they involve subjects that you can apply to your life, and the knowledge you gain from them can be implemented into the way you approach your goals.

- Biographies—These are great reads because they help you build courage. Oftentimes when you look at successful people, you only see the end results, and you fail to ignore the process it took them to get there. Biographies reveal the truth about what it takes to be successful. They show you what types of situations you may face on i path to living a purposeful life. When you read about someone who has accomplished something similar to what you want to achieve, you'll feel at ease knowing that they faced the same types of obstacles as you and had the same feelings that you're feeling.

If you're not a voracious reader, you should start out by trying to read at least thirty minutes per day. Multimillionaire and business coach Tony Robbins claims one of the things that made a huge impact on his life was making the decision to read at least thirty minutes per day. It may not seem like a lot, but over the span of the year, you can read twelve to fifteen books.

Once you get more comfortable with reading regularly, you can turn it up a notch. You can start to read a book per week. After you've done that, you can read a book every two or three days. The faster you're able to learn, the better. The knowledge you build on a daily basis will help inch you forward to the destination you're seeking.

Even if your interest is in one particular area, you should learn about all different types of subjects. You have to become eclectic in your knowledge. The reason for this is that everything is related. A common problem in academia is the lack of interdisciplinary teaching. Members of different departments are stuck in their ways of thinking and don't like to collaborate with the other departments.

In the book *Where Good Ideas Come From,* Steven Johnson talks about the concept of the adjacent possible. Every time you learn something new, you're adding to the adjacent possible. Basically, this means that you have the ability to open a new door in your mind.

Having knowledge of different subjects opens more and more doors. Many discoveries and inventions happened on accident. The inventor was looking to solve one problem, and as a result, he found the solution to an entirely different problem.

You never know when the information you gather is going to come in handy. It's a good idea to have a basic knowledge of different subjects so that you can make connections between ideas.

The reason you have to adopt a commitment to lifelong learning is because you're going to need a deep level of knowledge in order to be the best at what you do.

When you're in school, you're taught to have a superficial level of knowledge. You learn enough to past the test, and then you forget the information afterwards. This is why many people have problems getting ahead. They're level of knowledge is too shallow. What you don't know can harm you.

Some people are able to comprehend and retain information. This is the second level of knowledge. You're able to talk about the subject, and you have a decent understanding of it. This is one of the most dangerous levels to be at. If you stay at this level and fail to learn more deeply, you run the risk of becoming a dilettante.

A dilettante is someone who knows just enough to be dangerous. This type of person is easy to spot. They're the type of person who carries strong opinions about subjects they really don't know much about. They're the type of person who will read a few articles about political policy or economics and decide that they know enough to run a country. They're good at talking, but they're not good at doing.

You need to reach the level of instinctual knowledge. At this level, you don't even have to think consciously. You have an intuitive sense and feel for the subject. You're an expert in your field.

Anders Ericsson is famous for creating the idea of the "Ten Thousand Hour Rule." According to this rule, you're not a master in your field until you've dedicated ten thousand hours of concentrated and focused practice to your skill. That's a lot of learning!

You will continue to improve on your way to mastery. You don't have to wait ten thousand hours to become skilled. You will be much further along after the hundredth hour, and even more so at the thousandth. The key take away here is that you never stop improving.

The sooner you realize the depth of what it takes to become successful, the better your life will be. You have to learn every single day. There's no way around it. Do you have what it takes to put in the hours?

The Theory of Nothing

You now know that in order to be successful, you're going to have to commit to a life of continuous learning. There's another component that goes hand in hand with learning. When you're able to combine the two, the results can be powerful. I'm going to use an example of a wildly successful person to illustrate this superpower.

In the film *The Theory of Everything*, the life of the highly regarded physicist Stephen Hawking was portrayed. The movie showed his gradual deterioration due to his ALS, and it was inspiring to see how he overcame incredibly difficult circumstances and revolutionized the world of science. What pushed him to reach great heights and overcome his debilitating disease? If there were one word I could attribute to his success, it would be this: curiosity.

He was an infinitely curious person. You would have to be in order to seek a theory that describes everything in the universe. He challenged much of the conventional wisdom in the scientific community. At times, he was scoffed at and told that his theories were only pipe dreams, but the movie shows that later on his ideas proved to be the new model to follow scientifically.

The main thing I want to emphasize is how curiosity can help you reach great heights. All of the great thinkers in history were extremely curious people. They looked at the world as it was and pondered on what could possibly be done to change the world and also people's perception of it. Every invention, from things such as the light bulb, the automobile, the airplane, and many others were products of curiosity and imagination.

I see a lack of curiosity in the world today. Many people are simply moving through time, going through the motions, and keeping busy or entertaining themselves. I call this way of thinking and living "The Theory of Nothing."

We go through our formal education, and then once it is complete, the learning stops forever. As children, we were extremely curious and more than willing to learn. Take a look at children when they are intrigued and fascinated by something unfamiliar; See how their eyes light up with passion, excitement, and interest. Then take a look at adults who are just going through the motions; their eyes are devoid of passion, excitement, and interest.

The word *education* comes from the Latin *educe*, which means, "to draw out." It seems as if our education system is doing the exact opposite. It is based on the assumption that children aren't naturally intelligent and that they need to be taught by a force-feeding of information, through a rigid set of guidelines and tedious tasks, in order to learn. I believe that the only thing they need is an environment that is conducive to learning, and the children will flourish on their own.

If you're not careful, the education system can beat the curiosity out of you. It turns learning into a tiresome chore. By the time most of us reach adulthood, we are so tired of learning, and we are ready to adopt "The Theory of Nothing."

We go to work during the day, usually doing something that is minimally engaging for most of us, and then we go home, sit down on the couch, and watch TV for hours. We don't ponder how to improve the quality of our lives. We don't look up to the sky and fathom the infinite vastness of the universe. We don't do much of anything really.

The minute you lose your curiosity for the world around you the game is over. You run the risk of becoming stuck in your circumstances and resigned to your fate. You stop thinking of innovative ways to improve your life. You start believing that "it is what it is." Don't allow this to happen to you.

Rule number one is to always be learning. Rule number two is to always be curious. When you expand your imagination and let your curiosity flourish, you realize that there are endless opportunities in life. You'll see the world around you in an entirely different way. Instead of being resigned to your fate, you'll start thinking of ways to create a different reality for yourself.

My challenge to you is to get back the curiosity that was stolen from you in your childhood. Get into a state of deep thinking about your life and what it means to you. Do all of the things you want to do in life, so you have no regrets. Explore your mind and seek out ways to be innovative with your life. Use your curiosity to fuel your train on the track to destiny.

Successful Friends vs. Unsuccessful Friends

A key part in developing good thinking habits is being observant. You have to have a high level of awareness and notice what's going on around you. If you're trying to figure out how to be successful, there are clues everywhere you look. You just have to know how to find them.

A great observation exercise is the successful friends vs. unsuccessful friends strategy. The idea is to observe the difference between your successful friends and you're not so successful friends.

When you start to look, you realize that there are differences between successful people and unsuccessful people. Notice how each type carries themselves. How do they walk? How do they talk? What type of attitude do they have towards life?

I've noticed that my successful friends are always trying to become better. They read a lot, attend seminars, take courses, and do anything they need to do to improve. They spend their time talking about ideas instead wasting time gossiping. They're focused. They have a defined purpose for their lives. They're confident, not cocky. They're humble and willing to listen to other people who are more successful than they are. They're always curious. The more they learn, the quieter they get. They realize that there's a lot to know, so they spend more time listening than they do talking.

I've noticed my unsuccessful friends spend almost no time trying to become better. They like to complain. They blame their circumstances on the government, their employer, or anyone else beside themselves. They want a better life, but they're not willing to become better people.

They feel entitled. They think that life somehow owes them more, but they're not willing to give more. They think they know everything. They don't spend enough time learning. They don't read. They like to waste time on things that aren't important. They're not curious. They're going through the motions. They enjoy gossiping.

They're the type to scoff at people more successful than them. They say things like "They're just lucky." or "I could have done that if I were in their position." They talk a big game about what they're going to accomplish, but they never actually do anything.

The more you observe these differences, the clearer picture you'll have on what's going to lead to the destination you want and what's going to steer you away from it. You have to surround yourself with positive people and stay away from insecure and negative people.

Your group of friends has a big impact on your life. I'm not saying you have to completely cut people out of your life, but I promise you that keeping insecure and negative people close to you is going to cause problems.

People who are insecure can be envious towards you, and they will actively undermine your success and try to sabotage it. They're like crabs in a barrel. When a group of grabs are in a barrel and one tries to climb out, the others will grab it and pull it back down. People can be the same way.

If you're not careful, the people around you are going to try to drag you down because they know they don't have what it takes to be successful. They can't move up to your level, so they have to bring you down to theirs so that they won't feel bad.

You have to protect your mind. You might think you'll be able to block out the negative influences with sheer will, but it won't happen. You're senses can't block information they receive. You can tell someone you're not going to listen to them, but if they yell directly in your ear, you have no choice but to hear it.

People are going to try to distract you and throw you off of your game. When you're on the rise, people will notice. Some will congratulate you, but others will become naysayers. They'll tell you that you're crazy for trying to do something great. They'll tell you that what you're doing isn't going to work. They'll talk behind your back. You can't let this bother you.

Now that you're able to spot the differences between your successful friends and your unsuccessful friends, you have to decide which one of them you're going to be like.

Think

Reality is created in the mind. Your reality is based on your perceptions. Your perceptions are formed by what you think. The ability to think can be the most powerful asset you have. The best way to solve your problems is to think about solutions and innovate your way out of them.

"All of humanity's problems stem from man's inability to sit quietly in a room alone."—
Pascal

Oftentimes, people will feel frustrated and wish that they had a different set of circumstances. They resign themselves to their fate, and they never come up with a way to change their conditions. This is primarily due to the fact that they haven't taken the time to really think about what they can do about it.

Don't be one of those people. Instead, you should always be thinking ahead and planning your next move. You have to engage in chess-like-thinking. When a chess player makes his first move, he already has possible counter-moves in mind for the various ways that his opponent may come at him. He's not just thinking about the next couple of moves; He's thinking about the next ten to fifteen moves. You have to think the same way about your life.

Some people say you should live in the present moment, and there's some truth to that. You don't want to miss all of the little moments that life has to offer. But at the same time, you don't want to get too caught up in the day-to-day routine and lose sight of your vision. You have to keep your dreams and goals in the front of your mind every single day. Your imagination is going to take you further than anything else.

In the book *Where Good Ideas Come From,* Steven Johnson explains that many of the world's greatest innovations were not just moments of complete serendipity. Many of these innovators' ideas came to them in a form of a slow hunch.

A slow hunch is a lingering thought. You have a very vague idea in your mind, but you can't quite grasp it fully. It's always in the back of your mind, and you can't get rid of it. This is something you should pay attention to. If there's an idea that seems to stick with you for a long period of time, it's probably worth exploring.

Always have a notebook with you so that when you think of a good idea, you'll have it recorded instead of trying to memorize it. You should always be thinking of ways to revolutionize your life.

Every moment of your life is material. You might be a book chapter or conversation away from a life changing idea. You have to stay aware and try to make connections between everything and everyone you interact with. Don't think of your life as it is right now. Use your imagination to create a vision of how you want things to be in the future, and use your brainpower to find an innovative way to get there.

One of the best ways to use chess-like-thinking is to take some time each day to think. You might be saying to yourself, "I think all day. What do you mean take time to think?" I mean that you should find a quiet place where you won't have any interruptions and think.

Think about your goals for the future. Think of the next ten steps you need to take to get where you want to go. Think of the potential pitfalls in your way. Think of ways you'll be able to overcome them. Think of any and every scenario. Picture yourself in the future having everything you want. Capture that feeling and use it as fuel to keep you motivated.

Another useful way to help you think is to use the power of inversion. Inversion means thinking about what you don't want to happen. Instead of thinking about the things that are going to make you successful, think about the things that will make you fail, and don't do them.

Here are some examples of what not to do:

- Be envious—Instead of focusing on yourself and what you need to do, spend all of your time tearing down people that are more successful than you. Use that energy that could contribute to your success, and waste it on worrying about what other people are doing. Be a hater. Most unsuccessful people are haters.

- Make excuses—Instead of realizing that you are the common denominator in all of your problems, simply blame everything and everyone else for your problems. Even though deep down you know that you could be working harder, just pretend it's not your fault that you aren't where you want to be.

- Refuse to change—Do the same thing over and over again and expect different results. That is the definition of insanity.

- Don't learn anything new—Do not pick up a book for the rest of your life and acquire no new skills. Become obsolete by paying no attention to current affairs.

- When you get knocked down, don't get back up - When you face a little adversity, get a tummy ache and resign your life to a stand still. If you fail once, never try again.

- Worry about what other people think— Let other people's fears and limitations be imposed upon you. Suffocate in the opinions of others and drown in their sea of negativity.

- Surround yourself with losers—Refuse to cut bad influences out of your life.

> Surround yourself with unsuccessful people.

Those examples illustrate the power of inversion. Always remember to invert, invert, invert. It's the easiest way to get what you want. Sherlock Holmes used the method of inversion to solve his cases. He would consider every possible suspect and rule him or her out until there was only one left. You can do the same with your life. Rule out every negative outcome until you're left with success.

Removing Disabling Ignorance

You have to be able to build knowledge to bring you closer to your goals, but at the same time, you have to remove disabling ignorance from your mind. Disabling ignorance includes thoughts that are counteractive to success and limiting beliefs and rules you make up in your mind that have no bearing on reality.

People make up phantom rules for life because it makes them feel better. It takes the responsibility away from them and places the burden on outside circumstances. They create a story for their lives, and they live by it.

Intuitively, they know these rules are made up, but after a while, due to what's called confirmation bias, they begin to truly believe them. There are many made up rules people use to limit themselves, but here are a few that I thought of:

- The only way to make money is through a job.—I placed this at number one because it is the most illogical of all of the rules. You may not be built for a life of serial entrepreneurship, but you can find a way to turn your passion into profit. It may not be feasible for you quit your job right way, but there's a way to do something you enjoy in your spare time and make a business out of it.

- You have to go to college to be successful.—Many owners of successful businesses did not graduate with a college degree. Thomas Edison died with more than one thousand patents; he had an eighth grade education. Many people believe that a college degree will be something equivalent to the golden ticket in the movie *Charlie and the Chocolate Factory*. For many, the reality is an entry-level salary that is less than the tuition they paid, a mountain of debt, and a shrinking amount of job prospects. College is a useful tool, but it isn't the only way.

- You need a ton of money to start a business.—Some people seem to have the idea that you always need a large amount of capital to start a business, but this is simply not the case. In this age of technology, you're capable of creating a small empire with a laptop, a couple of dollars, and a dream.

- You can't pursue your dreams because you have a family to take care of.—This one is tough, I know. Having a family, and a household to take care of can be overwhelming. It seems like you barely have enough time for anything, let alone pursuing a new goal, but it can be done. It may be harder than usual, but it's worth it. You have to find the time for it. To get what you want, you have to deserve what you want.

- You have to be dishonest to make a lot of money.—People make up a multitude of different reasons for why successful people made it to the top. They must have lied, stolen, or cheated to get there. Obviously, there are some unscrupulous people in the business world, but that is not an accurate representation of all wealthy people. Do you want to know why the owners of successful businesses have so much money? It's because of you, the consumer. You buy their products and use their services. You can complain about how much money these business owners make, but you won't take a stand and live self-sufficiently like the Amish, will you?

- You have to be realistic.— I wish this word was deleted from the English language. Can you explain to me what realistic is? Who is the ultimate authority on what the measuring stick is for reality? This is a very limiting rule people make for themselves. Perception is reality. The only person stopping you is you.

- It's impossible.—The probability of things is variable, of course. Some things may even be considered improbable. However, if you took some of the modern technology we had and presented it to the people who lived one hundred, two hundred, five hundred, or one thousand years ago, they would probably accuse you of sorcery and witchcraft. You are the one who decides what's possible and what's not possible. The only limits on what you can create are self-imposed.

When you live your life by a set of imaginary rules, you're setting yourself up for mediocrity at best. If everybody played by the rules, society today would be much different.

The creators of the future are the ones who are blind to these so-called rules. If you want to live an uncommon life, you're going to need an uncommon approach, which means that you're not going to have any rules at all. When you don't have any rules, you're flexible and adaptable. You're going to need to be in order to deal with any obstacles you come across along the way.

You have to remember that knowledge isn't power. *The application of knowledge is power.* You can't just read a bunch of books, watch TED talks, and listen to podcasts and expect to become successful. You have to put your knowledge to practice and use it to create tangible results in your life. Remember what we talked about in the beginning. To get what you want, you have to deserve what you want. Never forget it.

You've learned the importance of learning as a lifelong habit. You've also learned to sharpen your thinking skills and become more observant. You've learned how to remove our limiting beliefs and use your thinking power and imagination as fuel to push your forward. In the next chapter you're going to create a plan to reach your destination.

For free bonus material visit:
www.thedestinyformula.com/bonus

Chapter 4:
Make Your Plan. Follow Your Plan.

In this chapter, I will show you how to create a plan that will narrow your focus and maximize your potential. You will also learn how to set realistic time frames for success and learn how to pace yourself on your journey. At the end, I will leave you with the proper focus to use going forward.

One Thing at a Time

When people set out on a path to reach their destination, oftentimes they are too scatterbrained. They want to do too many things at once. You have to be focused in order to get what you want, and to be focused, you have to have a narrow vision of what tasks are required in the present to benefit you in the future.

You might believe that multitasking is a beneficial skill, but it's not. Multitasking just means that you are doing a bunch of different things poorly or mediocre at best. The best way to get results is by focusing on one thing.

In the book *The ONE Thing* by Gary Keller and Jay Papasan, they detail the strategy of focusing on one thing at a time in order to reach a desired result. In an early section of the book, he describes the effects of geometric progression using dominoes. If you start with a domino that's two inches tall and continue to line up dominoes that are one and a half times larger than the previous one, the fifty-seventh domino will be as high as the moon! And in theory, you would be able to knock all of those dominoes down with a flick of your finger on the first one.

This is how you need to structure your plan. The reason most people never make any progress is because they think of the grandiose dream that's towards the end of the road, and it just seems too daunting to put in the work to get there. Set your goals in a way that makes you focus only on what's required of you in the present. That way, you have one area to focus all of your energy on, and you don't worry about the next step until you are done with the one at hand.

The most important part is picking your first domino. The 80/20 principle states that a majority of your results come from a small portion of your actions. You have to figure out what is going to give you the most bang for your buck. Time is your currency. You have limited amounts of time and energy to use, so it's important that you focus on the right area.

Keller and Papasan suggest picking one desired outcome for each stage on your path. You begin with the end in mind and reverse engineer the actions needed until you figure out what you need to be doing right now. The question they suggest you ask yourself is, "What's the ONE thing I can do today for [whatever you want] such that by doing it everything else will be easier or even unnecessary?"

This question helps you to focus and maximize your results. Trace the path backwards from your end goal and pick one thing for each stage in the journey that needs to be done.

- Someday goal—What's the ONE thing you want to do someday?

- Five-Year Goal—Based on your someday goal, what's the ONE thing you can do in the next five years?

- One-Year Goal—Based on your five-year goal, what's the ONE thing you can do this year?

- Monthly Goal—Based on your one-year goal, what's the ONE thing you can do this month?

- Weekly Goal—Based on your one-month goal, what's the ONE thing you can do this week?

- Daily Goal—Based on your weekly goal, what's the ONE thing you can do today?

- Right Now—Based on your daily goal, what's the ONE thing you can do right now?

All credit goes to Keller and Papasan for this strategy. I wanted to share it with you because it's a brilliant way to reach the results you want. The strategy works. I used it to write this book.

If you want do something challenging like writing a book, the wrong way to go about it is to open up a word document and just start typing. You have to have a plan. The end goal is to write the book, but you break it down into smaller pieces and action items. You do ONE thing at a time. It makes the process much easier.

Remember the advice from Charlie Munger—
"Slug it out one inch at a time day-by-day."

The base hit strategy is another method to give
you the right perspective on how to set goals.

Most people never get anywhere near the goals
they are trying to achieve simply because their
goals are too grandiose. They're always trying to
hit "home runs." If you're a hitter and your goal
is to hit home runs all of the time, you're going to
swing at everything thrown your way, and you're
going to have a low batting average. A smart
hitter knows when to wait for the right pitch and
focuses on getting on base. You have to be
patient in the same way when searching for
opportunities.

Get This Wrong and Pay the Price

You're reading this book because you want
something more from life. You realize that the
path laid out for you by others isn't the one you
want to take. You want to be successful. You're
motivated and ambitious.

All of this is great, but you'll get nowhere if you
get this next piece of the puzzle wrong. You have
to be able to set realistic time frames. One reason
why people don't succeed is because they don't
understand this concept.

If you're broke right now, you shouldn't expect to be a millionaire overnight, but this is how some people think. They are subject to the idea myth. The idea myth is that all you have to do is think of a really cool idea, outsource all of the technical aspects, and sit back and collect your money. This is not how creating a business works.

If you are overweight right now, you're not going to be a fitness model anytime soon. Yet people continue to buy books that tell them how to "Lose 30 Pounds in 30 Days."

The people who market these books know that they wouldn't sell very many that were titled "Lose a Pound and a Half Every Week for the Next Eighteen Months Gradually."

The media wants you to think that being successful is something that happens overnight.

In the book *Managing Oneself* by Peter Drucker, he suggests measuring your progress every eighteen months. Also, remember the "Ten Thousand Hour Rule" from earlier, and the fact that it takes many people years, or even a decade or more, to become successful.

Set a time frame that works for you, but make sure it's realistic. This all comes back to deserving what you want. It's going to take patience to get where you're trying to go. There will undoubtedly be moments of tedium and frustration along the way, but it will be worth it in the end. You have to follow the path of mastery.

Your brain is wired to want things to come easily. The reason why most of us never reach any of our goals is because we get frustrated early on in the process and decide it's not worth the effort. The time is going to pass either way. Why not use it to build a life that you're proud of?

There are two different options you can take. The first option is to take the easy way out. You decide that you're just going to follow the prescribed path. You're going to work for someone else and build their dream instead of building your own. You'll go to work everyday and wait for the weekend where you'll only have two days to really enjoy yourself then it's back to work. You'll likely have to do this for forty to fifty years. Then you'll get old and die. I painted a bleak picture to help you realize how big of a mistake it is.

The second option is the seemingly hard way. You decide that you're going to do what ever it takes to live a life that's built around who you are. You'll make a plan for your future and stick to it no matter what.

It may take you a few years, maybe even a decade or two, to reach the level you're aiming for, but you realize it's worth it. You grind it out every day. Some days are going to suck. Some days you're going to feel like throwing in the towel, but you won't.

You'll start to see your life changing, and you'll become more confident. You'll reach your destination, and you'll realize that the end result is not what makes you happy. You'll realize that the memories you created along the way are what make you happy.

You get to look back on your life with absolutely no regrets. Even if you never quite reach where you're trying to go, you don't have to deal with the lingering feeling of what could have been.

There are no shortcuts. You have to do the work. I'm sorry if you were expecting some sort of foolproof success strategy that will make you wildly rich overnight. If there were a get rich quick scheme out there that was verified to work, then everyone would be doing it. There are ways to speed up the process, but you have to pay the price.

Every truly successful person has paid the price. You see them on a magazine cover and think about how their life is right now, but you fail to realize what it took them to get there.

If you don't want to take the time to build a life you're proud of, then you should stop reading this book. In fact, you should throw away all of your books because they won't be of any help to you.

Be Quick but Not in a Hurry

Patience is a virtue when it's used correctly. Sometimes patience can be your greatest downfall. There are two different ways that people use patience. The first way is the one most people use, and it gets them nowhere. The second way is the one that successful people use to move towards the destination they're seeking.

The first method is called being patiently impatient. The patiently impatient person is the type who is always putting things off. He or she is patient when it comes to getting started. This is the path that leads to "should've, could've, would've, but didn't." The patiently impatient person is always full of excuses as to why they haven't done any of the things that they truly want to do. They'll say things like "I'm too busy." or "It's just not the right time."

There will never be a right time to get started. There's a great analogy for this way of thinking. If you had to wait until all of the lights turned green at the same time before you started driving, you would never go anywhere.

I know how it feels to want things to be perfect before you start. There can be some anxiety involved in trying something new. You're worried that it's not going to work. You're not looking forward to the frustrating parts of the process to come. If you're unable to move past your fear and take action, you will always remain stuck. In fact, the greatest cure for fear is taking action.

Here's an exercise to help you learn to take action: The next time you have something difficult to do that you're not looking forward to, jump right in and start doing it. Before you know it, the task will be completed, and it will help you build a healthy habit for the future.

The patiently impatient person is also the type who quits before they can get good at anything. When he or she finally gets around to taking action, he or she becomes frustrated easily and gives up before making any real progress.

"You act like mortals in all that you fear and like immortals in all that you desire."—Seneca, On The Shortness of Life.

Don't act immortal in all that you desire. Stop thinking you have time. Realize that your

life can be taken away from you at any moment. Do something about it.

The patiently impatient person doesn't fully grasp the importance of getting started until it's too late. This is the type of person who goes through a midlife crisis. He or she has been going through the motions for decades, putting off all of their bucket list items, until one day, they're in a state of panic because they realize how much time they've wasted.

"The graveyard is the richest place on earth, because it is here that you will find all the hopes and dreams that were never fulfilled, the books that were never written, the songs that were never sung, the inventions that were never shared, the cures that were never discovered, all because someone was too afraid to take that first step, keep with the problem, or determined to carry our their dream."—Les Brown

Hopefully by now, you're ready to take action. Instead of being the patiently impatient person, you're going to be impatiently patient.

The impatiently patient person takes action. Instead of worrying about how they're going to accomplish something, they jump in and get started. They don't suffer from paralysis of analysis.

The impatiently patient person realizes the importance of getting started and has the ability to make the commitment to being patient during the process because he or she knows that consistency is the key to success.

If you're taking on a new path, things are not going to be easy right away. You have to learn. You have to be diligent. You have to practice. You have to be *patient* during the process.

The only reason people are successful is because they make a commitment to do what ever it takes for however long it takes until it gets done. That's it. It's not about luck. It's not about genius or talent. It's about work and commitment.

You can read all of the self-help books in the world and create a positive mindset. You can listen to audios and watch TED talks until you're a Rolodex of affirmations and quotes about positivity. But you're not going to accomplish anything until you take action.

Don't get caught in the trap of thinking that having information is equal to taking action. There is no secret to success. The steps you need to take to be successful are right in front of you, and you know it. You can't positively think your way to the top. There's nothing wrong with gaining motivation from outside sources, but at some point, you're going to have to motivate yourself.

Many people think the world owes them something. Nobody owes you anything. It's great that you're a nice person, but there are a lot of nice people in the world. It's time to stop being self-centered and thinking that good things should happen to you for no other reason than the fact that you're you.

Persistence pays. If you make a commitment to be patient and stick with things until they pan out, there is a high chance that you're going to get where you need to go. Yes, it's true that sometimes no matter what you do you there is still the possibility of failure, but you have to push forward anyways. Are you ready to take action now? I'm going to assume you are. Next, we're going to talk about how you should focus your action and get the ball rolling.

Direction and Momentum

Two important areas you need to focus on during your journey are direction and momentum.

Planning and goal setting are valuable, but you have to be careful not to get locked into a rigid way of thinking about the journey. I'll tell you right now that things aren't going to go exactly as planned. Not even close.

You have to continue to adapt and deal with things as they come. Be flexible about the journey and obstinate about the destination. You always want to head in the right direction.

The best thing about direction is that it can be changed in an instant. You can't change your circumstances in an instant, but you can alter the course of your life at any moment.

Think about the complexity and intricacy of your life. Think about all of the small decisions and events that led to where you are now. You're never going to have complete control over what happens, but you can control your decisions. Your decisions act like a compass, pointing you in a certain direction with each decision you make.

Being successful is a decision. It's a choice. You have a choice every day to work hard or be lazy, to be persistent or to quit, to listen to the naysayers or believe in yourself.

Imagine your life five years from now if you continue to do the same things that you did during the past five years. Do you like that picture? If not, it's time for you to point your life in a new direction.

I learned this concept from the famous life coach and business strategist Jim Rohn. He says that, "Five years from now you will arrive, but the question is where?"

Think about it. Picture how your life will be five, ten, or fifteen years from now if you *really commit* to the process of improving. Years of learning, implementing, and experimenting are going to add up to something great.

The world isn't lacking passion, but passion is useless without commitment. The diligent person is rare. The patient person is rare. The determined person is rare. You have to be rare.

If you don't commit to the process, you'll end up like everybody else. You don't want to be like everybody else. The masses of men and women lead lives of quiet desperation. I'm not saying they're unhappy, but they're not living to the fullest. They experience a dull stress and pain because deep down they know that there's more to life than just existing. Work five days a week, have a tiny bit of time for fun, wash, rinse, repeat.

You're going to take control of your direction and use momentum to bring you closer to your dreams. Building momentum is powerful. You have to create a snowball effect. Your goal starts out as a tiny little snowball that's rolling down a hill. It keeps rolling and gets a little bit bigger as it goes down the hill. After a while, it really starts to grow to a substantial size, until one day, it's so huge that anything in it's way is getting obliterated.

Self-confidence comes from doing the things you set out to do. To create momentum, you want to use the base hit strategy we discussed earlier and continue to enjoy small victories day in and day out.

I'll use the example of becoming healthy through exercises to illustrate. You can't go to the gym a few times and become a body builder. At one point, that herculean, stone chiseled, ridiculously strong body builder that you glare at during your gym sessions had to start out lifting the bar with no weights on it.

He's probably been lifting weights for several years, maybe even a decade or two. There are no shortcuts. He had to go there and get stronger, little by little, day by day, for a long time.

As time goes on, however, going to the gym gets easier. You may be sore for a week after your first time, but after a while, you begin to build momentum. The stronger you get and the healthier you feel, the easier it becomes to go back to the gym every day. You may even look forward to it. This same concept of momentum building can be applied to any area of your life.

If you have never been in business before, you won't make a million dollars next month. First, learn what it takes to make it in your industry. Spend a lot of time learning and reading. Find a mentor to work underneath or beside you. Then maybe you can strike out on your own.

If you've always wanted to become a great golfer, it probably isn't a great idea to immediately start playing at Pebble Beach. Going to a driving range, playing consistently, and finding courses that match your skill set is a more likely route to finding eventual success. The same methodology can be applied to any situation or goal.

The great thing about building momentum is that it's not linear; it's exponential. The increases are gradual at first, but sometimes you are able to take massive leaps forward because you've built a solid foundation.

You can take a pick and chip away at a stone one thousand times, and it won't make a single indent. Then the very next time it may shatter completely. This is how success works. Step-by-step you get ahead but not necessarily in fast spurts. Build momentum and prepare yourself, and when its time to run, you'll be fit for the sprint.

We all see the professional sports team win the championship at the end of the year, but perhaps we forget that for them, the season started in training camp or in the workout programs during the off-season. The team isn't elated simply because they've earned the crown; it's because they remember all of the *work* it took them to get there.

The reality is that you simply need to do the things you know you should be doing. There's no secret, and there's no substitute. You have to become better each day, and you can't ever let up. It's simplistic, and in a world that seems to be over complicated, perhaps a simple approach is what we all need.

If you slug it out inch-by-inch, day-by-day, and are fortunate to live long enough, *you will get what you want.*

You've learned to use the ONE thing strategy to maximize your focus. You've also learned how to use realistic time frames to set the right pace on the path to reaching your goals. You now know the importance of focusing on direction, building momentum, and creating a snowball effect. In the next chapter, you're going to learn about some ways to deal with the emotions you're going to encounter on your path.

For free bonus material visit:
www.thedestinyformula.com/bonus

Chapter 5:
Dealing With Obstacles

In this section, you're going to learn some helpful ways to deal with the inevitable setbacks and roadblocks that you will come across. You will learn the importance of using perception to see things as they are. You will learn about negative attitudes to avoid. You will learn how to manage your expectations and always be ready for what's to come. You will also learn how to deal with adversity and develop a persistent attitude to push forward until you get what you want.

It's All About Perception

The path you walk is not going to be an easy one. The way you handle yourself during your journey will determine how far you make it.

The first thing you need to learn how to do is control your perception. Perception is the lens you use to determine your reality. Everybody has his or her own unique way of viewing things.

Each of us is living in a different reality that's shaped by our thinking.

This is a concept that's hard for some people to grasp. When you're dealing with a situation that's not ideal, you can feel like life is *happening to you,* but the truth is that you are choosing to feel a certain way about what's happening to you. The events themselves don't determine how you feel about them.

"Things are neither good nor bad, but thinking makes them so."—William Shakespeare

Think about it this way. There are things that offend certain people but don't bother others whatsoever. If you put ten different people through the exact same scenario or situation, they'll act ten different ways based on their perception. You have the power to shape your reality.

The difference between happiness and sadness comes from the story you tell yourself about your life. We all have our own standards for the way we think our lives should be. If we fall short of those standards, we are unhappy. You should have high standards for your life, but you don't need to create a story where you'll only be happy if you get everything you want in exactly the way you want it.

You can perceive your journey as long and arduous and get discouraged easily, or you could view it as a process that requires one step at a time. You can dread the work, or you can focus on each step and enjoy the process of creating a new life for yourself. Each option is derived from the same "reality," but they're viewed in different ways.

Your perception comes from your philosophy on life. In order to change your life, you have to change your philosophy. Here's an example of a philosophy that will lead to a less than stellar life:

Life is unfair. I'm a good person, and I deserve more than what I have right now. I don't make enough money at my job. They should give me a raise. The government isn't giving us enough help. They should do more for me. I would try to start something on my own, but when you have a family and bills to pay, it's just not an option. Those successful people are greedy. They must have cheated or worked the system to get where they are. If I had the same lucky breaks as them, I would be successful too.

Successful people have a different philosophy on life. Successful people have a philosophy similar to this:

The world is an amazing place full of endless opportunity, and it's my job to take advantage of it. I know that if I continue to learn and improve myself, good things are going to happen. I have to put in the work. Nobody is going to just hand me success. Anything that happens along the way will make me better because I will learn from it. I believe that success is inevitable for the people who have the guts to stick it out.

You have a choice to decide what things mean. The world can be an unfair place, or it can be full of opportunity. You can worry about things that are out of your control, or you can focus on yourself and let the things on the outside take care of themselves. It's up to you.

The good news is that as long as you're alive, you have unlimited opportunities to change your mind and your perceptions. The bad news is that if you wait too long, you can run the risk of having a hardened mind and become locked into a certain way of thinking. Continue to have a poor philosophy for too long, and it can be extremely difficult to change it.

You see people like this all of the time. They decided a long time ago what the story of their life was going to be.

People often use the term *reality* as if it were this autonomous entity that each individual happens to be a part of. Reality only exists in your mind. Everything you think is real is only real because you think it is.

If you want a different reality, you can create it in your mind. It might not appear in tangible form right away, but a vision coupled with diligence and effort will lead to prosperity.

When an architect is planning to build a house, she doesn't start building it until she has a blueprint. She has to see the house in her mind before it can exist. You build a life in the same way. You have to take care of your mind and control your perceptions to make it on the path to finding your destiny.

Diseases of Attitude

This next section will elaborate on controlling your perceptions by talking about some attitudes and emotions that will trip you up if you're not careful. They are what business philosopher Jim Rohn refers to as "diseases of attitude." You must avoid these at all costs.

- Self-Pity—Feeling sorry for yourself won't do anything to help you live a better life. Self-pity paralyzes you and leaves you unable to take any action towards improving your situation. There is a distinct difference between acknowledging that you're not where you'd like to be and feeling sorry for yourself. One leads to doing something about the problem, and the other leads to the problem worsening.

- Neglect—A week of neglect can cost you a year of repair. Neglecting to take care of your financial situation can lead to a perilous outcome that can be difficult to climb out of. Neglecting your physical health increases the difficulty of regaining it over time. Neglecting your relationships may mean losing them altogether. Pay attention to the things that are important in your life because failing to do so can have disastrous results.

- Indifference—You're neither hot nor cold. You don't care at all. You're drifting through life with a directionless sail that will lead to an undetermined destination. You can't drift your way into prosperity. To be successful in anything, you have to actually give a damn about it. Pick a direction and go for it with everything you have. Even if it's the wrong direction, at least you'll find out quickly. The best way to live is one way or another, not in the middle. If you're inspired, you will have the energy to move mountains. If you're desperate, you will have the energy to fight your way out of your circumstances. If you're indifferent, you are destined to live in metaphorical limbo for the rest of your life.

- Indecision—You can't make up your mind as to what to do with your life. You struggle with choosing a path that's right for you. Indecisiveness keeps you in exactly the same position you've always been in. Leaders have to be able to make decisions, and if you're not able to come to a decision quickly, you can't be considered a leader. A life of adventure is filled with many decisions. The decisions that turn out to be incorrect help to give you better perspective going forward and provide you with valuable experience for future decisions.

- Doubt—There are several types of doubt, but self-doubt is the most damaging. You doubt if you're good enough, smart enough, or talented enough. You doubt if you're able to reach your goals, and even when you find success, you doubt if it will last. If you don't believe in yourself, the game is over before you even begin playing. Success comes from faith and self-confidence. The understanding of self-worth is the beginning of progress.

- Worry—Incessant worrying has a negative impact on your mental state as well as your physical state. Worrying doesn't solve anything. Worrying too often can reduce you to being the type of person who is doomed for the rest of your life. Give it up. Eradicate it from your life completely. Removing worry is a liberating experience. It doesn't remove difficulty, challenges, and obstacles from your life, but it allows you to be much more capable in facing them.

- Over Caution—You're afraid to take any sort of risk whatsoever. You say to yourself, "What if I try and fail?" or "What if it doesn't work?" You only highlight the risks involved instead of looking at the rewards. The penalty for not trying at all outweighs the penalty for trying and failing. You should fear risking your sanity for a life of presumed safety and security. You should fear risking living a life filled with regret. Either you join the game or stand on the sidelines and watch the winners play. The choice is yours.

- Pessimism—The glass is always half empty. You go out of your way to find the negative in any and every situation. Spending your whole life looking for potential reasons why things won't work is a sure fire way to be unhappy. Your mind is like a field, and your thoughts are like seeds. Your mind doesn't care what you plant; it will grow whatever seeds you decide to sew. When harvest time comes, you will reap what you've sewn in abundance. Poor thinking habits lead to living a poor existence.

- Closed-mindedness—You think you know everything. You're the type of person who loves to spout your opinions yet doesn't want to hear anyone else's. You think you have life all figured out. Epictetus said, "It is impossible to begin to learn which one thinks one already knows." Instead of having a know-it-all approach to life, become more curious. Open your mind to new ways of thinking, new types of people, and new experiences. It's nearly impossible to live a great life with a closed mind and a hardened heart.

- Complaining—Whining, crying, bitching, moaning, groaning. It goes by several monikers. I saved this one for last because if you don't get rid of this one, you have a zero percent chance of having an excellent life. Complaining kills dreams with an assassin-like efficiency. You complain about the weather, your job, your partner, and your kids; you complain about everything. Shut up. Stop it. Cut it out. Knock it off. Don't cry about your life. Do *something about it*.

Managing Your Expectations

There's a caveat to this process. Although you may do everything right and follow the steps necessary to reach your goals, you can still fall short. Some things are just out of your control. The key to having durability and persistence is to manage your expectations.

I want you to have a gigantic vision for your life in the long run, but at the same time, you should actually err on the side of being a bit pessimistic in the short run. Too many people fall into the trap of believing that positive thinking alone is going to lead to the desired result, when this couldn't be further from the truth.

There are books like *Think and Grow Rich*, which say you just need to have desire and purpose and everything else will fall into place. There are plenty of people with desires that go unfulfilled.

What you really need is a plan that allows for contingency. You need a strategy. You need to see potential roadblocks that you may encounter. You need to be single-minded yet agile. You need to adapt. You need to prepare for the worst and hope for the best.

There's a strategy you can use to map out possible outcomes and create a plan for each outcome. There are three likely scenarios that you're going to encounter when you are striving to reach a goal or desired outcome.

The first scenario is that you're going to be wildly successful. You're going to hit the bull's eye and achieve everything you want. Your friends will praise you, and your naysayers will envy you. For this scenario, you plan your celebration. I'm sure this won't be too hard for you to do.

The second scenario is that you fall flat on your face. The business you start goes bankrupt. The book you write sells zero copies. You don't get anywhere near the desired result. Before you decide to try to accomplish something, you have to keep this scenario in mind. You have to decide beforehand if you're going to be able to handle a massive defeat. You have to be ready to dust yourself off and start all over again. This is the difference between the winners and the losers.

The last scenario is something in between massive success and massive failure. This is the most likely scenario. In this scenario you reach a moderate amount of success, but you could have done better. Your business makes a profit but has room for growth. Your book sells a decent amount of copies but it could have sold more.

In this case, you should plan your next move using the information you gain from this venture. You can refine the process and attempt to do even better the next time.

Your business will grow because you have a better idea of what to do going forward. Your second book will be a hit because you've taken the knowledge from the last attempt and you will use it to make the next one better.

There's nothing wrong with incremental success. In fact, this might be the best way to build towards a long-term vision.

You might not want to become too successful right away. If everything works out exactly as you planned on your first try, you might develop the false assumption that everything you touch turns to gold, when in reality, you just got lucky. If you happen to fail in the future, it will be devastating because you won't be prepared for it.

Your goal is to use your talents and strengths to share something with the world, so eventually you're going to have to do that. Before you decide to share it with other people, go through a checklist of potential things that can go wrong. In doing this, you can tweak some parts of your strategy so that you're able to avoid potential mistakes.

This ties in with the chess-like-thinking I told you about earlier. It's fine to enjoy life in the present moment, but you also have to keep your eyes peeled at all times for what's to come. You may not know what the future holds, but you have to do your best to be prepared for anything.

You have to be confident, but not arrogant. Confidence comes from having a plan that you follow diligently and consistently. Hubris comes from thinking that you're going to be successful for no other reason than the fact you're you.

You must believe in yourself, but that belief has to be founded in some form of effort. You can believe that if you continue to work, learn, and grow that you will be successful, but it's foolish to think that success is guaranteed just because you want it badly.

This is the reason why many businesses fail. They're not based on solid business practices. They're based on overconfidence and arrogance. They build products that nobody wants. They lack awareness of the world around them and don't see the signs of impending doom that they're destined for. You have to be better.

You should have crazy and ambitious goals in the long run, but in the short run, you have to watch out for danger.

Dealing with Adversity

You have to learn how to deal with the inevitable obstacles that will present themselves in the future. Obstacles are almost guaranteed to try and get in your way of success, and they're what cause most people to give up on their dreams. You are different. You are going to follow the strategies in this book and use them in your life to overcome obstacles. You are not going to come this far just to fold when things get a little bit difficult.

There are several different ways to deal with obstacles.

You can look at an obstacle that you're trying to overcome like Mt. Everest. You can stand at the bottom and look up in awe at the challenge that lies ahead of you. This approach will make it almost certain that you will fail. When you place an obstacle in a context that makes it seem insurmountable, you will be defeated psychologically before you even begin. This is what many people do when they attempt something substantial.

I remember multiple times where I tried to write a book in this fashion. Instead of focusing on what I needed to do to get started, I would think about how hard it is to write an entire book, and I would be too discouraged to make any progress.

The way you need to approach an obstacle is by figuring out what you need to do first, second, third, and fourth, until you overcome what's in front of you. You need to "line up your dominoes," and focus on the first task at hand to create the momentum needed to topple the rest of the dominoes.

That's the process I used to finally finish and publish this book. I started by brainstorming and mind mapping what I wanted to write about. Then I created a detailed outline for the book. I focused on writing each section of the book one at a time. I didn't get wrapped up in thinking about the finished product. I wrote a new section of the book every single day until the first draft was done.

You're going to have setbacks along the way to accomplishing something of value. Your character reveals itself when you're under pressure and face a challenging situation. How you react to obstacles you face will determine how successful you will be. The most important thing you need to remember is that *it's supposed to be hard.* The hard is what makes it good.

Instead of trying to fight the grind, you have to learn to love the grind. If you want and expect things to come easily with no hiccups or problems, you're delusional.

The reason why life can be so hard at times isn't simply because it's hard. It's because of the idea it's not supposed to be. Maybe the reason so many of us are unhappy isn't because our lives are necessarily bad, but that we have unrealistic expectations of what life is supposed to be like.

No matter what happens in life, it moves forward, and what's done is done. Things aren't always going to go your way, and nature doesn't care about your meticulous planning for the future. When faced with an unexpected setback or obstacle, you have two choices:

1. You can dwell on it, brood, and let the weight of your problems overwhelm you.

2. You can step back, analyze the situation, and make a plan to push through it,

jump over it, walk around it, and learn from it.

When something you planned goes wrong, you can use it as an opportunity to learn something valuable for the future. Any other way of dealing with obstacles is futile.

In the book *Bounce* by Matthew Syed, he talks about a figure skater that is trying to learn a difficult spinning axle move. She repeats the process over and over again, falling on her butt with each failed attempt. She never got discouraged about the failed attempts because she believed that each failed try brought her closer to getting the move right.

The most successful people in the world know that the path to success comes through failure and not by trying to avoid it. Don't get me wrong. You don't want to fail just for the sake of failing. You should always try to make your attempts successful, but it's likely not going to happen perfectly.

It doesn't matter how successful you become. You are always going to have to deal with a new obstacle or challenge. You should look forward to them. You should realize that they are going to help you grow and make you better.

You build muscles by creating resistance. The resistance causes your muscles to tear themselves apart and put themselves back together. Treat your obstacles like mental exercises. You might face situations that will tear you apart, but if you're able to put yourself back together, you'll be ten times stronger than you were before.

Don't let life simply happen to you. Do something about it. Once you start giving up and letting your problems weigh on you, it's the beginning of the end. You see people like this all of the time. They are constantly complaining about their lives and doing absolutely nothing about it.

I'm not saying that life isn't hard or that it's completely fair. It's not fair in the sense that some people face more difficult situations than others, but it is fair in the sense that there are enough available resources to dig yourself out of any situation.

If life deals you a bad hand, you can decide that it's not fair and complain, but then what? It doesn't change anything or make it better. You can live in misery, or you can create a strategy and iterate your way to success.

Treat your obstacles like your teachers. Learn from them. Get better because of them. Flip them on their head and use them to solidify your resolve and strengthen your character.

The Marathon Mentality

The journey you're traveling on is a marathon and not a sprint. You've already learned the importance of being patient, but it's such a critical factor that I need to reiterate it's importance. You need to run your race at a steady pace in order to be successful. When you treat your journey like a marathon, you're setting yourself up to succeed by using consistency.

If you're a runner and you have 26.2 miles to run, you're not going to start sprinting right away, yet this is what people do when they try a new way of doing things.

They're very excited in the beginning, but after a few frustrating moments and set backs, they're done for. It's because they wanted things to come too quickly, and they didn't take the time to learn.

A marathon runner has to run at a pace that's much slower than a person who is just running one mile. They have to stay focused on each step to keep going forward. The process is grueling at times. They might feel like they want to quit, but they don't.

Taking things step-by-step will prepare you for fast spurts. There will come a time when there's an opportunity that can be seized, but it's of no use if you're not prepared. Success comes when preparation meets opportunity.

This is not to say that you can't make improvements in the short run. You do want to make progress as you go, but just remember that rushing is going to probably do more harm than good.

Persistence pays major dividends. We've already helped you discover a path that's built around who you really are and that's based on your talents and strengths, so your success is inevitable if you do things the right way.

Your success is inevitable if you never stop learning. Your success is inevitable if you're diligent. Your success is inevitable if you're humble. It's not inevitable without your effort.

In any successful person or company, you see the end product of persistence, diligence, and consistency. Sure, there are some people who go from rags to riches quickly by finding a great idea that spreads like wildfire. But what is the likelihood that you're going to be the next Mark Zuckerberg? Those types of stories are one in a billion.

There are countless stories of self-made individuals who made it to where they are now through persistence and diligence as opposed to having a flash of brilliance that made them successful overnight.

Stop chasing mirages. The sooner you get rid of the idea of the overnight success, the better off you will be. If you have the belief that you are going to stumble on a great idea that's going to change your life immediately, you might as well just buy lottery tickets.

There are going to be points where you will feel like giving up. It's okay to feel frustrated, but it's not okay to give up completely. The difference between people who get where they're trying to go and people who don't is the ability to stick it out. That's it.

You've learned how to shape your reality using the lens of perception. You have also learned how to avoid negative thinking. You've learned how to prepare for different scenarios as well as tempering yourself to deal with obstacles in order to stay the course.

We're going to wrap up the book by giving you some attitudes that you can use to be successful going forward, but they won't matter unless you make a decision to stick it out no matter what happens. Decide right now that you're going to start on your marathon and run until it's done.

For free bonus material visit:
www.thedestinyformula.com/bonus

Chapter 6:
Attitudes For Success

To end the book, I will leave you with some successful attitudes that you can carry with you for the rest of your life. I will give you my definition of success and also give you some ways to think about your success on a personal level. I will tell you how to elevate your game and make success chase you. I will tell you how to face your fears. Lastly, I will tell you the one thing that all successful people have in common.

What Is Success?

In order to talk about success, we first have to define it.

Success is a word that's often attached to things like material possession, fame, and notoriety. Although those are some consequences of living a successful life, those types of things aren't what make you a successful person.

To me, being successful means that you get to wake up everyday and do exactly what you want to do. It's having the freedom to live a life that's based on who you really are, not who you're told to be or think you should be.

It's having a life that serves a purpose greater than your individual needs. It's being able to provide a value to the world that only you're capable of providing. It's the ability to share your truest self and shine brightly without shame. Success is the ability to think for yourself and be yourself every minute of your life.

This is why it's important to build a life that's based on who you really are. You can make a lot of money in a profession that's not true to who you are and still not be successful. Sure, you may have the outward trappings of the type of success that's defined by society, but you're trading away your precious time, which is more valuable than money.

Life doesn't have to be short. Life can be long if you're able to find a way to spend your time appropriately. Life only feels short if you've spent the majority of it doing things that you don't enjoy.

I think that's the main reason why many people are unhappy. They are stuck in a reality that doesn't seem to fit their truest selves. We are brought up to believe that life is supposed to be a certain way, and we can end up blindly following this prescribed path without stopping to think if it's truly the right way to go.

To be successful, you have to block out the noise of the world and figure out what's best for you. You have to know yourself and listen to yourself to follow the right path.

It's not necessarily a given that you know yourself either. You're being influenced by outside forces that are trying to tell you who you're supposed to be, what you're supposed to want, and how you're supposed to act.

Many people have lost sight of who they really are, and they're living a life that's nothing more than the patchwork of the opinions and beliefs of the society they belong to. It takes effort to discover who you really are and make your circumstances fit your vision of life.

I've given you my definition of success, but the truth is that being successful ultimately comes down to living up to your personal standard of what that word means. Success takes on a different meaning depending on who you ask, but the one thing that each person has in common is that they want to capture a certain feeling. The definition of happiness is living a life that's in line with the way you'd like it to be.

Success isn't about doing everything right; it's about doing the right thing. It's establishing a few disciplined actions that you repeat every day. If you make a plan for your future and follow the steps accordingly, then you are successful. If you can look in the mirror and be satisfied with the amount of effort you're putting forth, then you are successful. If you're better than you were yesterday, then you're successful. The definition is up to you.

Make Success Chase You

You've probably heard phrases that tell you to chase your dreams and go after what you truly desire. These types of statements lead you to believe that success is something that is sought after, but a better approach is to think of success as something that chases you, not the other way around.

Success is something you attract by the person you become. You have attracted your current circumstances by the person you are right now.

Your philosophy on life determines the type of person you are. The type of person you are contributes to the decisions you make on a daily basis. The decisions you make have an impact on your circumstances.

Many people like to treat their circumstances as something separate from themselves. They place the blame on their circumstances when in reality the conditions of their lives have more to do with their philosophy and character than anything else.

Remember in an earlier chapter we talked about rich friends and poor friends. Your rich friends most likely have a positive attitude combined with a thirst for knowledge. They've become the type of people who attract success because they have developed skills and become more valuable.

Your poor friends are most likely opinionated, unwilling to learn, and lazy. They have attracted negative circumstances to their lives because of their bad attitudes. It's rare to find someone who is committed to self-development that ends up being a failure in the long run.

The best way to find success is not to look for it. Instead, you must continually work on yourself and elevate your game to a level that's so high that the circumstances you want have no choice but to fall into place.

"Be so good they can't ignore you."—Steve Martin

When you develop yourself and become more confident, you won't feel like you have to chase after success. You will realize that you have something to offer the world and that the world has no choice but to recognize you because you're that valuable.

How do you become so good they can't ignore you? By getting better every day. Remember that developing skills and building knowledge is not linear; it's exponential. When you go to bed a little wiser than you were when you woke up day after day, you will reach a point where your skills and talent level start to make dramatic increases. Your continual dedication to self-improvement will create a snowball effect that will make you unstoppable.

If you're diligent and take things one-step at a time, there's no need to worry. You shouldn't be in a hurry because as long as you decide to stay the course, your success is inevitable.

Michael Jordan is the perfect example of elevating one's game. He never worried much about who his opponent was. He was only in competition with himself. He knew that he put in more effort during practice than any other player in the league, so he had the confidence to destroy his competitors on the court.

People marvel at his high flying dunks, but they miss the fact that he perfected simple basketball moves and shots that built a rock solid foundation for the rest of his game. Even the greatest basketball player of all time took a step-by-step approach.

You probably would have many of the things you desire right now if you had been diligently working for the past eighteen months. Now is your time to decide that you're going to stop making excuses and start elevating your game.

All successful people understand their role in the events of their lives. They understand that nobody is responsible for their level of success except for themselves.

To get what you want, you have to deserve what you want. There's no way around that sobering fact. Are you going to take responsibility for your own success?

"Don't wish it were easier; wish you were better. Don't wish for less problems; wish for more skills."—Jim Rohn.

There are three types of people in this world. There are people who make things happen, people who watch things happen, and people who wonder what happened.

The people who watch things happen are the ones who sit on the sidelines and gossip about the people who are actually making things happen.

The people who wonder what happened haven't taken the time to build knowledge, so they're clueless to what's going on.

The people who make things happen don't have time to worry about what others are doing. They're on a mission to get better. Which one are you?

What You Should Really be Afraid Of

You want to be successful, but there is one word that can potentially hold you back and keep you from living out your destiny. That word is *fear*. When it comes to the pursuit of a dream that seems a bit lofty and unrealistic, fear is the underlying emotion that causes many people to either give up or fail to get started in the first place.

In order to reach success, you have to be able to conquer your fear and even use it to your advantage. The truth is that there are definitely some things that you should be afraid of, but they aren't the type of things most people usually fear.

We live in a fear based society. Instead of living glorious, exciting, and liberating lives, many of us are doing life in an imaginary prison we've created for ourselves. Fear is the locking mechanism, yet we are the only ones who have the key. Here are some things you shouldn't be afraid of but probably are.

- What other people think of you—It seems that many of us spend the majority of our time doing things for the approval of others rather than the fulfillment of our own wishes. We are scared to death to fall flat on our face in front of a crowd. You shouldn't be afraid of what people will think of your decision to follow the path you were meant for. The people who you seek approval from are probably just as insecure as you.

- Failing—You were raised to fear failure. If you didn't reach a certain mark in class, you were subject to scorn and ridicule. This fear extended into your own household where the people who you love the most (your parents) might scold you for not living up to certain standards. Your upbringing is literally a process of conditioning you to fear coming up short. As cliché as it may sound, you can overcome failure, and as long as you're alive, you can try again, and again, and again. You get unlimited chances under one condition: you have to be breathing. Many of us give up after one attempt. To be successful, you have to embrace failure instead of fear it.

- Change—This mental diversionary tactic blocks you from reality. It's called loss aversion. You cling to what you already have, and you would rather stay stagnant than lose the ground you've gained. In order to get what you want, you must be able to adapt. It's not the strongest or smartest who thrives; it's the ones who are able to pivot on a dime when necessary. One strategy you attempt may not work, and you will have to ditch it and go back to the drawing board, over and over again, until you get it right.

- Being different—Conformity is comfortable. It's safe to live in anonymity in a sea of average people. Standing above the crowd takes courage. To live in a way that diverges from the conventional wisdom will lead to resistance from others. When you try to stand out, some will envy you, and they may actively work against you. People want you do to well but never better than them. You can't be pinned down by the fears and limitations of other people. Their problems are not yours, and there is no need for you to shrink and shrivel just to make them feel better.

Many of us are worried about things that probably don't deserve the time of day. At the same time, there are some things that we should be absolutely terrified of but pay no mind to whatsoever. Many of us don't realize it until it may be too late. Here are some things that are actually a little bit healthy for you to be afraid of:

- Wasting your time—Many of us are frugal with our finances and wouldn't give away our hard earned money to other people for no reason, yet we seem to have no problem being generous with our time. We spend hours on Facebook, watching television, or doing other things that provide no value to our lives. You can lose all of your money and find a way to get it back, but when time is spent, it's gone forever. Treat your time preciously. We live as if we have all of the time in the world. In reality, every day can actually be our last.

- Aging (in a certain sense)—We as a society fear aging, but perhaps it's for the wrong reason. For most of us, this reason is a cosmetic one; we fear looking older and becoming less desirable. You should be afraid of aging simply because your drive decreases with age. You just won't be able to muster up the same amounts of energy you were able to when you were younger. I'm not saying it's impossible to succeed if you are older, but it gets more difficult as time passes.

- Losing your momentum (getting stuck)—Momentum is a key driver of success. The worst thing you can do is become stagnant. I'll use the example of fitness again to illustrate my point. The more out of shape you become, the harder it is to get back into shape. This same way of reasoning can be applied to your life.

- Settling—The enemy of great is good. I'm not sure if trying for something big and failing is as regretful as never shooting for the stars and having to live with the fact that *you never tried*. This is sort of a dull pain that continues to linger throughout the lives of many people. This is also the reason why some people love tearing down successful people. It's their way of slyly building themselves up. They would rather slander those who took some risks and made it big than face the fact that they just didn't have the guts to attempt it themselves.

- Spending your life doing things that you don't want to do—Think about it. You get to do this whole life thing one time. One time. The universe has been around for billions of years and will continue on infinitely. What you do here doesn't really matter in a sense, so why put so much pressure on yourself to live a certain way? Live how you want to live. Your biggest fear should be living a bad life. You should be afraid of dying with regrets.

Alexander the Great said that there are two types of people in this world. There are those that conquer their fears and those who don't and suffer and die from them. The inability to conquer your fears will ruin your life. To be successful, you have to remove all of your self-imposed limitations and have the courage to follow through with what you set out to do.

You Have to be a Little Bit Crazy

To wrap things up, I will leave you with the most important advice I can give you to become successful in what ever you decide to pursue. In order for you to build a life you're proud of, walk the path you were meant for, and achieve everything you want to achieve, you have to be a little bit crazy.

"The people who are crazy enough to think they can change the world are the only ones that do."—Steve Jobs

Your problem is almost always going to be thinking too small. You need to have a gigantic vision for your future, and you have to believe that you will be able to make a dent in the universe.

You live in a society that wants you to believe in practicality and mediocrity. You have been told all of your life to play things safe and to avoid taking any risks. Does it seem like this way of thinking is working out for the majority of people?

You have to be crazy enough to believe that there's more to life than punching a clock and spending forty hours per week doing something that you don't really like at all.

You have to be crazy enough to believe that you can use your unique abilities to create a living for yourself and that you have the power to change your circumstances by getting better.

You have to be crazy enough to believe that you are capable of doing big things. Why not you? Why does it have to be someone else who gets to live it up?

You have to be crazy enough to believe that you have something that the world not only wants but also needs you to share. You have to believe that you hold an immeasurable amount of power within you.

You have to be crazy enough to believe that it's going to work. You need to have faith that you're going to be able to pull it off. You have to silence that nagging whisper of self-doubt that subtly tries to sabotage you along the way.

You have to be crazy enough to keep going even when the situation is looking bleak. You have to have the ability to endure set backs and continue to persist until you get it done. You have to be crazy enough to make one thousand attempts if need be.

You have to be crazy enough to decide that you're never going to quit no matter what happens. You have to be a little bit crazy to succeed.

For free bonus material visit:
www.thedestinyformula.com/bonus

Conclusion

By now you should be ready to follow the purposeful path that you were always meant for. It's my sincere hope that you do everything that you can to live the life you've always dreamed of. I wrote this book because I've always felt like there was more to life than being ordinary and I want to share that message with as many people as possible.

I'm glad that you've taken time to read the book, but what I really want you to do is take the necessary action to achieve your goals and turn your vision into reality.

Every single day your life is inching closer toward its end. You never know what day will be your last. That fact isn't negative to me; it's motivating. I want you to get the most out of your minutes, hours, and days so that you can be able to live life the way it's meant to be lived.

There are going to be times where you feel frustrated. There will definitely be times where you want to quit. I've been there. When you feel like quitting you can always go back to your *why* and focus on the reason you started this journey in the first place.

Think about your life in the long run. Every time you run into an obstacle or hit a stand still you have to remember that if you give up now, you're giving up your future.

Take some time to talk to some elderly people about their lives and the things they regret. I guarantee you some of them will say that they regret not taking any chances and following their dreams.

Don't wait until it's too late to realize how precious and short your time on this earth can be. No matter how old you are, the best time to start is now. Right now you're the youngest you'll ever be.

I truly believe that success is something that everybody can have. If you figure out what your strengths are and continue to develop them you will succeed. Don't worry about what other people around you are doing. Focus on your mission.

Like I said earlier in the book, persistence pays. Don't follow your passion. Work on your passion. Patience and diligence are what separate the mediocre from the great. What ever you're trying to achieve is possible if you give it enough time.

You get what you give in life. If you want to stay inside of your comfort zone and never take any chances that's fine, but don't expect to live a great life because you won't.

I know it can be scary to do something great, but you have to push through the fear and do it anyways. The fear doesn't ever go away, but you build more courage each time you're able to act in spite of your fear.

Make your plan. Follow your plan. Stay persistent and never give up. If you do that, you'll have everything you've ever dreamed of.

For free bonus material visit:
www.thedestinyformula.com/bonus

Resources

Drucker, P. (2008). *Managing oneself.* Boston, Mass.: Harvard Business Press.

Greene, R. (2012). *Mastery.* New York: Viking.

Holiday, R. (2014). *The obstacle is the way: The timeless art of turning trials into triumph.* Penguin.

Keller, G., & Papasan, J. (2012). *The one thing: The surprisingly simple truth behind extraordinary results.* Austin, Tex.: Bard Press. www.the1thing.com

Johnson, S. (2010). *Where good ideas come from: The natural history of innovation.* New York: Riverhead Books.

Munger, C., & Kaufman, P. (2008). *Poor Charlie's almanack: The wit and wisdom of Charles T. Munger* (Expanded 3rd ed.). Virginia Beach, Va.: Donning Pub.

Schwartz, D. (1987). *The magic of thinking big*. New York: Simon & Schuster.

Seneca, L., & Costa, C. (2005). *On the shortness of life*. New York: Penguin Books.

Sinek, S. (2009). *Start with why: How great leaders inspire everyone to take action*. New York: Portfolio.

Syed, M. (2011). *Bounce: Beckham, Serena, Mozart and the science of success*. London: Fourth Estate.

About The Author

Ayodeji has been known to read entire books in one sitting. He once read three books simultaneously, one chapter of each at a time, until he finished all three of them.

He did this in two days.

For as long as he can remember, he's always had a contrarian view of the world and the way that society operates.

In the past year Ayodeji has read more than 75 books on topics ranging from personal development, philosophy, psychology, spirituality, marketing, and sales.

He believes that lifelong learning is the key to being successful.

Ayodeji currently works in marketing and web design. He is also an author, personal development blogger, and entrepreneur.

You can find more of his work at:
www.thedestinyformula.com

For free bonus material visit:
www.thedestinyformula.com/bonus

Made in the
USA
Columbia, SC